DATE DUE

DEC 2 1 2012	
MAR 2 9 2016	
APR 1 2 2016	
OCT 1 8 2016	
NOV 10 2016	

PRINTED IN U.S.A.

WEAPONS OF WAR

TANKS
INSIDE & OUT

MICHAEL E. HASKEW

ROSEN
PUBLISHING®

New York

This edition first published in 2012 by:

The Rosen Publishing Group, Inc.
29 E. 21st Street
New York, NY 10010

Additional end matter copyright © 2012 by The Rosen Publishing Group, Inc.

Project Editor: Sarah Uttridge
Picture Research: Terry Forshaw
Design: Zöe Mellors

Library of Congress Cataloging-in-Publication Data

Haskew, Michael E.
Tanks: inside & out/Michael E. Haskew.
    p. cm.—(Weapons of war)
Includes bibliographical references and index.
ISBN 978-1-4488-5980-1 (library binding)
1. Tanks—History—Juvenile literature. I. Title.
UG446.5.H3733 2012
623.7'475209—dc23

2011030666

Manufactured in the United States of America

CPSIA Compliance Information: Batch #W12YA: For further information, contact Rosen Publishing, New York, New York, at 1-800-237-9932.

Copyright © 2010 by Amber Books Ltd. First published in 2010 by Amber Books Ltd.

Photo Credits: Art-Tech/Aerospace: 12, 19, 24, 30, 31, 49, 61, 66, 78, 84, 85, 136, 154; Art-Tech/MARS: 113; BAE Systems: 92; Cody Images: 4, 5, 6, 36, 43, 72, 73, 112, 148; Hans Halberstadt: 107; Krauss-Maffei Wegmann: 137; Narayan Sengupta: 55; Tank Museum: 13, 18, 25, 37, 42, 48, 60, 79, 101, 119, 131, 155; U.S. Department of Defense: 7, 67, 90, 91, 93, 94, 95, 100, 106, 118, 124, 125, 130, 142, 143; Wikimedia Creative Commons Licence: 54 (Caplio G3), 149 (Rama); All artworks courtesy of Art-Tech/Aerospace, Alcaniz Fresno's S.A. and Amber Books

Contents

Classic Tanks 1918–1960   4

Sturmpanzerwagen A7V	8
Mark V Male	14
PzKpfw IV	20
T-34/85	26
M4A4 Sherman	32
PzKpfw V Panther	38
PzKpfw VI Tiger	44
IS-3 Josef Stalin	50
Centurion A41	56
T-54/55	62
M48 Patton	68
M41 Walker Bulldog	74
AMX-13	80
M60	86

Modern Tanks 1961–Present   92

T-62	96
M113	102
Chieftain Mark 5	108
Leopard 1	114
AAV7	120
T-72	126
Leopard 2	132
M1A2 Abrams	138
Leclerc	144
Challenger 2	150

Glossary	156
For More Information	157
For Further Reading	158
Index	159

Classic Tanks 1918–1960

The tank debuted and matured rapidly on the battlefield, asserting firepower, mobility, and armor protection like no other land warfare system in history. From design to reality, it revolutionized the way in which wars have been fought.

A British Centurion tank, painted in a European camouflage scheme, awaits orders during exercises. Note the armor skirting for protection of the tracks and wheels against projectiles and land mines.

The concept of the tank, a virtually irresistible, indestructible, and intimidating engine of war, may be credited to Leonardo da Vinci and his fifteenth-century vision of a mobile, well-protected fortress. However, considering the sweep of history, it may also be asserted that the Greek phalanx, with hoplites grouped tightly together, their shields interlocked and bristling with spear points, is nothing short of a "human" tank.

TRENCHES TORN

Its origin notwithstanding, the tank came into its own during the recent, war-ravaged past. While the aircraft has reigned supreme in the skies and the battleship, aircraft carrier, and submarine have held sway on and beneath the sea, the tank has proven itself the mailed fist of the land battle.

The appearance of British tanks on the battlefield during World War I proved a shock to the German military establishment, and the response was swift. In a relatively short period of time, both the Allies and the Central Powers were assailing the enemy's lines in primitive tanks, belching bullets from machine guns or firing heavier cannon. Although the tank may have exhibited plenty of firepower, its most innovative aspect was that of mobility.

Static warfare, theorists reasoned, might well become a thing of the past should tanks be introduced in significant numbers. A modern war of speed and maneuver could result, placing an enemy's fixed defenses in peril. Perhaps more than its direct impact on the outcome of World War I, the earliest operational tanks such as the British Mark V and Whippet and the German A7V proved to be harbingers of things to come.

TANKS IN TRANSITION

British soldier and military strategist J.F.C. Fuller was among the earliest advocates of armored warfare during the twentieth century. His influence was reported to have spread and directly impacted the developing battlefield tactics that would define the tank in World War II.

A Churchill tank stirs up a cloud of dust along a dirt road. One of the most versatile chassis designs ever conceived, the Churchill served as the basis for a variety of specialized vehicles.

One tale of Fuller's armored perspective relates that the British officer attended a review of the burgeoning German army on April 20, 1939, the occasion of Hitler's 50th birthday. Fuller was said to have commented that for hours "a completely mechanized and motorized army roared past the Führer." Hitler supposedly remarked to Fuller as the review ended, "I hope you were pleased with your children." Fuller was reported to have responded, "Your excellency, they have grown up so quickly that I no longer recognize them."

Although this story may be apocryphal, it nevertheless illustrates the breadth of Fuller's influence on the strategy and tactics of modern armored warfare. A generation after the first steel monsters edged slowly across no-man's-land, the panzers of Heinz Guderian rolled across France to the English Channel, Erwin Rommel's Afrika Korps gained lasting fame, Bernard Montgomery's Desert Rats were victorious at El Alamein, George S. Patton's armored spearheads relieved Bastogne, and Georgi Zhukov's T-34s rolled through the streets of Berlin.

POST-WAR PROLIFERATION

During the Cold War, the world's great powers continued the development of tanks and complementary armored fighting vehicles that were capable of transporting combat infantrymen into action, delivering direct fire support, fording streams, removing the wounded and dead from the battlefield, providing anti-aircraft defense, and other supporting roles. The tank itself evolved during its first half century, serving as armored cavalry, a primary weapon of breakthrough and decision in battle, and the powerful projector of military might on land.

The T-34 medium tank, and those of the KV and Josef Stalin series, manufactured by the Soviet Union during World War II, were exported in

A column of M4 Sherman tanks pauses along a city street during an advance. The second tank in line has been upgunned with the 3-in (76.2-mm) 17-pounder, while the first mounts the original 2.95-in (75-mm) cannon.

Festooned with camouflage branches, an M113 armored personnel carrier rolls along as its crew focuses forward. The M113 has served as a troop transport and fighting vehicle for nearly half a century.

numbers to client states of the Soviet Bloc, nations of the Middle East, the People's Republic of China, and North Korea. These were followed by the export versions of the T-54/55 and others. In the West, Great Britain, France, and the United States developed powerful tanks based on their experiences during the war. The ubiquitous American Sherman and the British cruiser tanks, whose sheer numbers had overwhelmed the Tigers and Panthers of Hitler's panzer divisions, gave way to heavier designs of the late 1940s and early 1950s, such as the Centurion, Patton, and the AMX-13 light tank.

Through more than 40 years of alternating war and peace, the armored formation and its accompanying mechanized infantry developed into the modern war machine that was capable of decisive victory on land. A relative few future military operations on the ground, whether offensive or defensive in nature, would result in victory without the involvement of armored forces.

Eventually, the mere presence of tanks and armored fighting vehicles would dictate the course of most military ground operations.

"The fact that the tanks had now been raised to such a pitch of technical perfection that they could cross our undamaged trenches and obstacles did not fail to have a marked effect on our troops."

German Field Marshal Paul von Hindenburg
on British tanks during World War I

Sturmpanzerwagen A7V

Shocked by the appearance of Allied tanks on the battlefields of World War I, Germany hastened to develop an armored fighting vehicle of its own. The result was the Sturmpanzerwagen A7V, an ungainly steel fortress made mobile by a tractor chassis.

MAIN ARMAMENT
The main weapon aboard the Sturmpanzerwagen A7V was the Russian Sokol or Belgian-made Maxim Nordenfel 2.24-in (57-mm) short recoil gun, which was fired by a crew of two, a gunner and a loader.

SUSPENSION
The basic suspension system of the Sturmpanzerwagen A7V was that of the Holt tractor, an agricultural vehicle that included 30 small wheels. Components of the suspension system were produced in Austria.

SECONDARY WEAPONS
Six 0.31-in (7.92-mm) Maxim machine guns were situated in the rear and along the sides of the tank. A single "Female" variant, possibly chassis No. 501, was reportedly produced with an additional two machine guns forward and no heavier weapon.

DRIVERS
Two crewmen, positioned inside a noticeable bulge atop the center of the tank, were required to drive the Sturmpanzerwagen A7V, operating a steering wheel and a system of levers.

ENGINE
Two four-cylinder Daimler engines, mounted in the lower center of the Sturmpanzerwagen A7V, powered the vehicle, which weighed at least 30 tons (27 tonnes), at a top road speed of 9.32 mph (15 km/h) with 100 hp (74.6 kW).

ARMOR
The armored protection of the Sturmpanzerwagen A7V was 1.2 in (30 mm) to the front and 0.8 in (20 mm) on each side; however, the steel was not tempered and could not withstand large-caliber shells.

The A7V was designed by committee, meaning that everyone involved had a say as to the overall end product. A weapon designed by a committee usually tends to fall excessively short of expectations, as was the case with the gangly looking Sturmpanzerwagen A7V.

STURMPANZERWAGEN A7V

STURMPANZERWAGEN A7V – SPECIFICATION

Country of Origin: Germany
Crew: 18
Designer: Joseph Vollmer
Designed: 1916
In Service: March–October 1918
Manufacturer: Allgemeines Kriegsdepartement, 7. Abteilung, Verkehrswesen (German army)
Number Built: 21
Produced: October 1917–October 1918
Weight: 35.8 tons (32.5 tonnes)

Dimensions:
Length: 26.25 ft (8 m)
Width: 10.5 ft (3.2 m)
Overall Height: 11.5 ft (3.5 m)

Performance:
Speed: 5 mph (8 km/h)
Range, Road: 50 miles (80 km)
Range, Cross-country: 18 miles (30 km)
Power/Weight Ratio: 6.15 bhp/ton 1800 rpms
Ground Pressure: n/a
Fording Capacity: 2 ft (0.65 m)
Maximum Gradient: 30 degrees
Maximum Trench Width: 7.25 ft (2.2 m)
Maximum Vertical Obstacle: 1.5 ft (0.46 m)
Suspension Type: Coil-sprung bogies

Engine:
Powerplant: 2 x Daimler-Benz 4 cylinder in-line 165204 gasoline engines each developing 100 hp (74.6 kW) @ 1800 rpms
Fuel capacity: n/a

Armor & Armament:
Armor: 0.8–1.2 in (20–30 mm)
Main Armament: 1 x 2.24-in (57-mm) L/12 Maxim-Nordenfelt short recoil gun. 500 rounds
Secondary Armament: 6 (or more) x 0.31 in (7.92 mm) MG08/15 machine guns in flexible mounts. 18,000 rounds

Variants:
Sturmpanzerwagen A7V: Basic series designation.
Überlandwagen: Unarmored, open-top supply vehicle.
A7V/U: Proposed redesign with sponson-type all-around tracks.
A7V/U2: Proposed model based on the A7V/U, this one having slightly smaller track sponsons.
A7V/U3: Proposed "Female" version of the A7V/U2, having only machine guns as armament.

RIVAL: SCHNEIDER CHAR D'ASSAULT

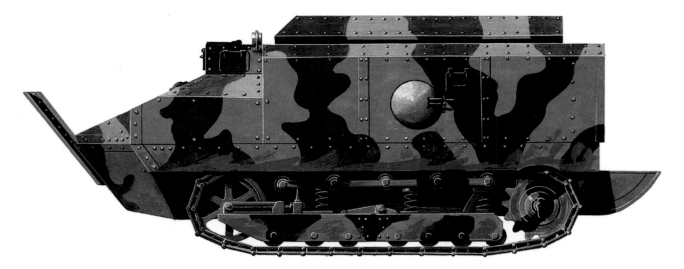

STURMPANZERWAGEN A7V

A captain in the German army and an engineer by profession, Joseph Vollmer headed the design committee that developed the Sturmpanzerwagen A7V. Although German tank design efforts had begun as early as 1911, the hurriedly produced A7V exhibited several notable flaws. At 10 ft 10 in (3.3 m) in height, its silhouette was quite conspicuous, while its ground clearance was only 1.6 in (40 mm). Traversing trenches or even depressions of any depth was virtually impossible. Its full complement of 18 crewmen included a commander, two drivers, machine gunners, and ammunition suppliers, as well as a gunner and loader for the 2.24-in (57-mm) cannon.

The first French tank, the Schneider (above) was designed by Colonel Jean-Baptiste Eugene Estienne and mounted a 2.95-in (75-mm) petard mortar. A second French tank, the St. Chamond (below), appeared months later and proved to be a disappointment.

RIVAL: CHAR D'ASSAULT ST. CHAMOND

Crewmen prepare three German Sturmpanzerwagen A7V tanks for deployment to the battlefield. Only 20 of these behemoths were actually delivered to the Western Front. A single example survives and is displayed at a military museum in Australia.

On November 13, 1916, Germany decided to build tanks. The new vehicle provided a universal platform, to be used as a base for both a tank and a cargo carrier. The first pre-production A7V was built in September 1917.

In the month following the initiation of Operation Michael, Germany's desperate offensive in the West launched on March 21, 1918, the first confirmed engagement in history between opposing tanks occurred near the French village of Villers-Bretonneux. Here, three German Sturmpanzerwagen A7Vs met three British Mark IVs, one of them the upgunned Male variant mounting a pair of six-pounder cannon. During the initial exchange of gunfire, the Female Mark IVs, armed only with machine guns, were damaged and fell back. The lone Mark IV pressed on, disabling one German tank, commanded by Lieutenant Wilhelm Biltz, and killing five of its crew as they exited the burning A7V.

Second Lieutenant Frank Mitchell, commanding the remaining Mark IV, began to withdraw. However, his tank was heavily damaged by a German mortar round. Seven British Whippet light tanks then advanced, but four of these were quickly put out of action. It is unclear whether the

remaining A7Vs engaged the Whippets or the light tanks fell victim to other German fire. The damaged A7V was later salvaged by the Germans, and it proved to be one of those that had entered combat on March 21. Of these, two were damaged when they fell into shellholes, three were captured by Allied troops, and others suffered mechanical difficulties.

OUTSIDE THE BOX

Designed and constructed as a box on a tractor, the Sturmpanzerwagen A7V performed best in stationary positions on level ground. Because these ideal conditions were seldom found on the Western Front in 1918, and only 20 A7Vs are known to have become operational before the end of the war, the tank failed to provide an adequate response to the British designs.

The thick steel plating of the A7V provided greater protection for its crew than that of its British counterparts. However, the vehicle's cramped quarters and limited maneuverability often left German crewmen preferring to enter combat in captured British tanks. Two variants, an open-topped supply vehicle, the Überlandwagen, and the A7V/U, similar in design to British types with all-around tracks and two 2.24-in (57-mm) guns, were built. A mere 75 of the Überlandwagen were completed, and the A7V/U reached only the prototype stage. The A7V was last employed in combat in October 1918.

IMPROVED DESIGNS UNAVAILABLE

Several improved German tank designs were in various stages of development at the war's end, but none were available before the armistice. The Treaty of Versailles compelled the Germans to research and develop new tank designs in secret in the interwar years.

In a note of supreme irony, the Sturmpanzerwagen A7V appears to have been conceived and constructed with its primary emphasis on firepower rather than maneuverability. As the progenitor of the highly mobile German panzer divisions of World War II, the A7V is hardly recognizable as the ancestor of the mailed fist of Hitler's Blitzkrieg a generation later. The only intact Sturmpanzerwagen A7V, No. 506, which was nicknamed Mephisto, is on display today at the Queensland Museum in Brisbane, Australia. Mephisto was one of the three Sturmpanzerwagen A7Vs captured at Villers-Bretonneux on April 24, 1918.

Interior view

The Sturmpanzerwagen A7V had space for up to 18 crewmen. The compartment housing the driver and the commander was centered on a raised platform above the fighting compartment.

(1) **Steering Wheel: The driver's seat was positioned to the left in the upper compartment, surrounded by controls.**

(2) **Clutch Pedals: Two clutch pedals were used to engage the gears of the transmission located below. These were located below and forward of the driver's seat.**

(3) **Speed Control Selector: This was set for three optimal speeds, 2, 4, and 7.5 mph (3, 6, and 12 km/h).**

(4) **Starter Hand Wheel: This was used to crank the two four-cylinder Daimler engines that powered the ponderous tank.**

(5) **Drive Levers: Two drive levers were operated independently, one for each track, to initiate forwards and reverse motion. A speed control wheel assisted with wide turns.**

(6) **Brake Levers: These operated independently, each track controlled by a separate system, and assisted in halting the vehicle.**

Mark V Male

Late in 1917, Great Britain began producing the Mark V Male tank. It saw limited service during World War I, primarily at the Battle of Hamel in the summer of 1918. The Mark V was a progression from the Mark I, the world's first combat tank.

DRIVER
The first tank that required only a single driver, the Mark V had a Wilson epicyclic gear-box. Seated at left, the driver manipulated levers to control the movement of the Mark V.

MAIN ARMAMENT
The heavy armament of the Mark V Male tank consisted of two 6-pounder artillery pieces mounted in sponsons on either side of the armored vehicle, while secondary armament included four Hotchkiss machine guns. The Female version of the Mark V was armed with four Vickers machine guns and two Hotchkiss instead of the cannon.

UNDITCHING BEAM
Carried on top of the rear of the Mark V was an unditching beam, similar to a railway tie. Chaining the beam to the tracks enabled the driver to extricate the vehicle from muddy terrain.

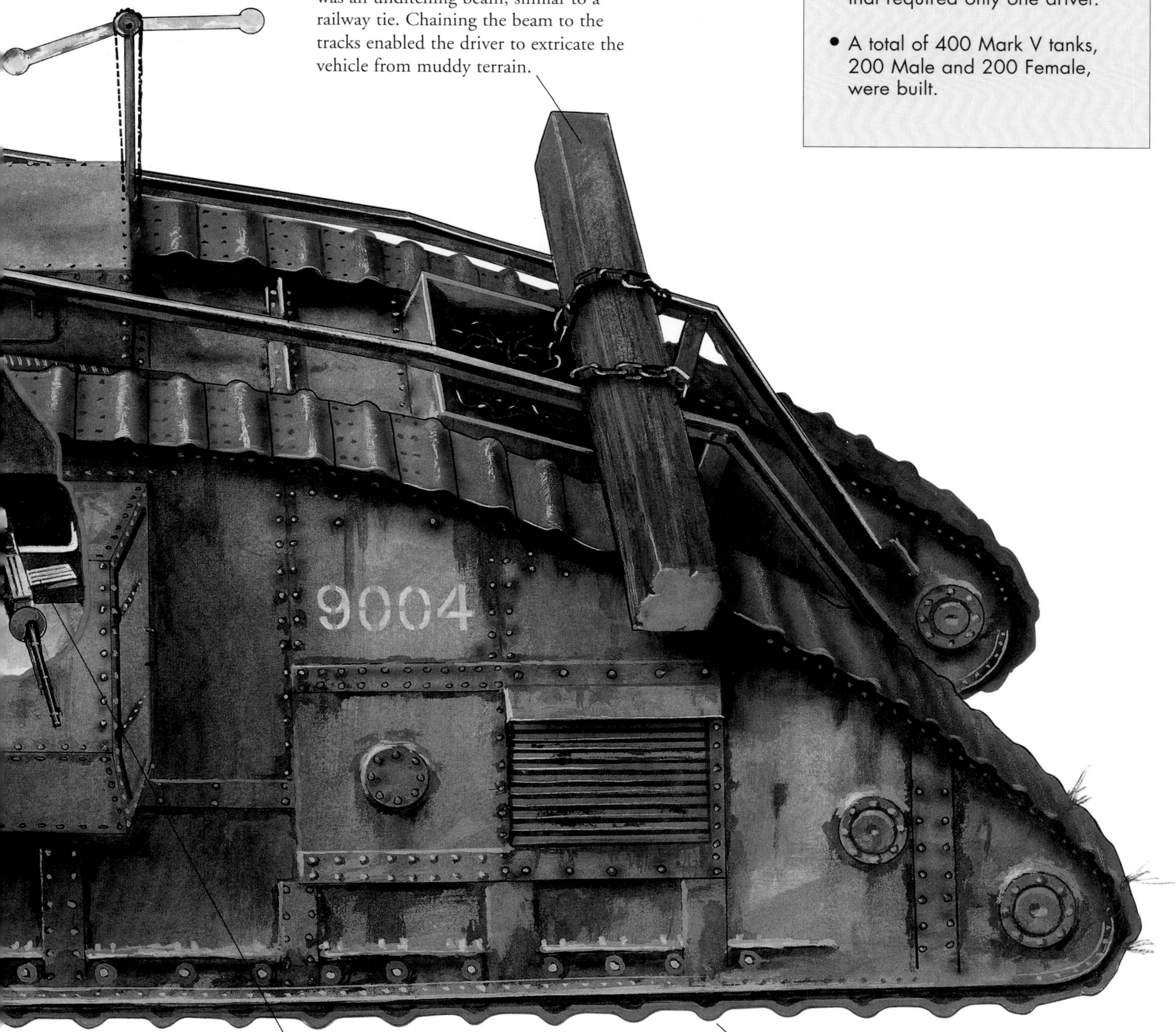

9004

MACHINE GUN MOUNTS
The Mark V incorporated the Skeens ball machine gun mount, which improved the traverse of the weapon from 60 to 90 degrees and offered increased protection from enemy fire.

LENGTH
The length of the Mark V was eventually increased more than 6 ft (2 m) beyond that of its predecessor, the Mark IV, to nearly 27 ft (8.5 m). This was to facilitate the crossing of German trenches, which were sometimes more than 3 ft (1 m) wide.

The Mark V Male tank was deployed late in World War I and so was involved in combat on a limited basis, serving with the British, French, Canadian, and American armies. Its actual length of service spanned the interwar years.

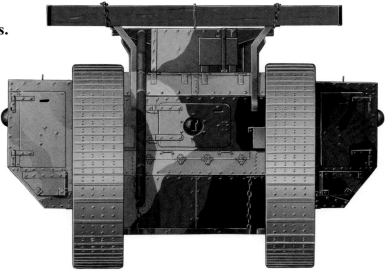

MARK V MALE – SPECIFICATION

Country of Origin: United Kingdom
Crew: Eight (commander, driver, two gearsmen, and four gunners)
Designer: Major Wilson
Designed: 1917
In Service: 1918
Manufacturer: Metropolitan Carriage
Number Built: 400
Produced: 1917–June 1918
Weight: 32.5 tons (29.5 tonnes)

Dimensions:
Length: 27 ft (8.5 m)
Width: 13.48 ft (4.11 m)
Height: 8.66 ft (2.64 m)

Performance:
Speed: 5 mph (7.4 km/h)
Range: 45 miles (72 km)
Power/weight Ratio: 5.2 hp/ton
Operational range: 45 miles (72 km), about 10 hours endurance

Engine:
Powerplant: 1 x Ricardo gas engine delivering 150 hp (110 kW)
Transmission: 4 forward, 1 reverse, Wilson epicyclic in final drive
Fuel Capacity: 100 imperial gallons (450 l)

Armor & Armament:
Armor: 0.24–0.55 in (6–14 mm)
Main Armament: 2 x 6 pounder guns in side sponsons
Secondary Armament: 4 x 0.303-in (7.7-mm) Hotchkiss Mk 1 machine guns

Mark V Variants:
Mark V (Male): 2 x 6-pdr guns; 4 x Hotchkiss machine guns
Mark V (Female): 4 x 0.303-in (7.7-mm) Vickers machine guns
Mark V*: Personnel Carrier; transport for up to 25 personnel; Male and Female variants available
Mark V:** Improved Tank Mk V* model; Male and Female variants available
Mark V:** (Tank RE)

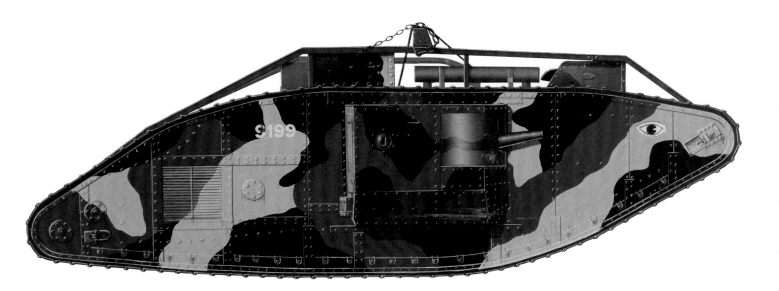

MARK V MALE

The Mark V Male tank provided added firepower with its two sponson-mounted 6-pounder cannon and four Hotchkiss machine guns, but its heavy weight of nearly 29 tons (26 tonnes) and ponderous track arrangement limited its operational range to 45 miles (72 km) and its single engagement timespan to about 10 hours. The 150 bhp (110 kW) Ricardo engine was difficult to start, requiring four men to crank manually while another pressed a magneto switch. In cold weather, personnel had to prime each of the six cylinders and warm the spark plugs. The Mark V crew of eight included a driver, two gearsmen, four gunners, and a commander.

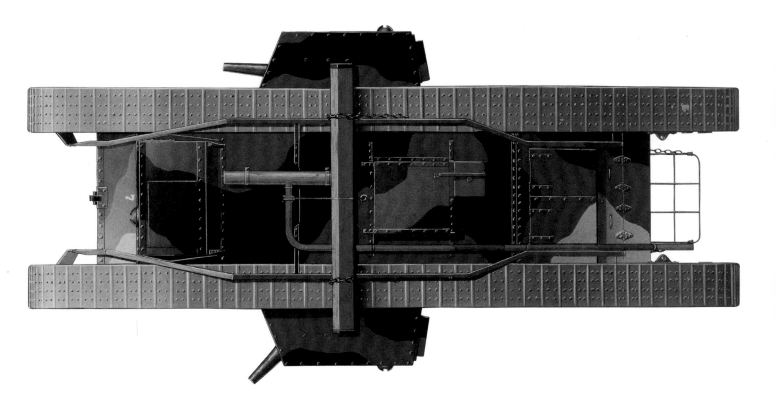

The Mark V Male opened ways through barbed wire and crossed trenches easily. Tanks and infantry adapted to each other's tactics. Infantrymen understood it was not essential for them to gather behind tanks because they could deploy in skirmishing order close to the tanks.

Although it was initially conceived as a completely new design, both the Male and Female variants of the British Mark V combat tanks actually developed as a vast improvement over their predecessor, the Mark IV. Following the debut of the tank on the battlefield at Flers-Courcelette in September 1916, the pace of armored vehicle development increased rapidly. By the end of World War I, no fewer than nine variants of the original Mark I tank participated in Allied operations on the Western Front.

Interior view

The British Mark V was the first tank that required only a single soldier as a driver. Seated forward, he viewed the battlefield through a slit in the armored hull.

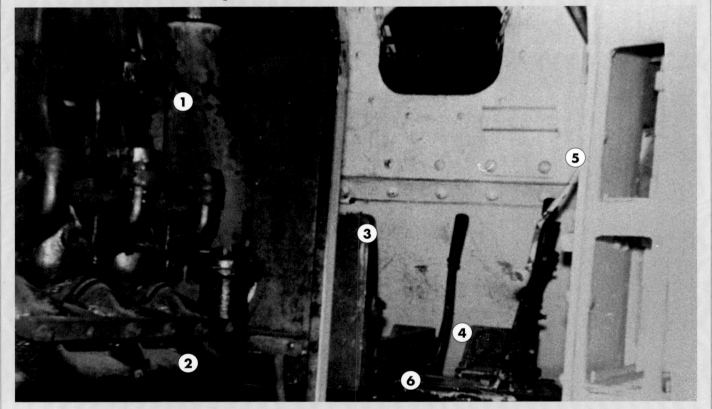

(1) **The Engine Compartment:** Here the 150-hp (110-kW) Ricardo gas engine, the first powerplant specifically designed for a tank, was housed.

(2) **Exhaust Manifolds:** These evacuated fumes to the outside. Crew were often overcome by the gases produced by enclosed engines.

(3) **Driver's Seat:** Located forwards and to the left with a machine gunner to his right. A gearsman was not needed in the Mark V.

(4) **Clutch Pedal:** This was operated to change the four forwards or single reverse gears of the Wilson epicyclic transmission.

(5) **Steering Tillers:** The driver operated the Mark V with tillers in forwards or reverse motion, as well as maneuvering through turns and cross-country.

(6) **Foot Brake:** This was readily accessible to the driver and responsive in halting the Mark V and assisting in changing direction.

British infantrymen inspect a curiosity of war, the Mark V Male tank, which represented a major advance in armored vehicle design and deployment. The Male version of the Mark V mounted heavier firepower than its Female counterpart.

The Mark V incorporated a number of improvements over the Mark IV, including the Wilson epicyclic gearbox, which required only one crewman rather than two to steer the nearly 33-ton (30-tonne) fighting vehicle. While the Male variant included a pair of sponson-mounted 6-pounder guns along with a complement of four 0.303-in (7.7-mm) Hotchkiss machine guns, the slightly lighter-weight Female Mark V was armed with four 0.303-in (7.7-mm) Vickers machine guns. These were fired by single crewmen from Skeens ball mounts, which improved the firing arc from 60 to 90 degrees and provided greater protection for the gunner than the earlier loophole or firing slit configuration of the Mark IV. The 150-bhp (110-kW) engine designed by Harry Ricardo generated greater speed than the Mark IV, and the addition of an undetching beam assisted in navigating soft terrain.

IN ACTION

The combat debut of the Mark V took place on July 4, 1918, as Australian and American troops assaulted a salient in the German line at Le Hamel. Sixty Mark Vs of the 5th Brigade, Royal Tank Corps, supported by four supply tanks, attacked with the infantry. One Australian soldier commented that the presence of the tanks did not relieve them of their sense of obligation to fight and that the soldiers did take immediate advantage of every opening created by the advance of the tanks.

The Allied thrust achieved its objective in a mere 93 minutes, and General J.F.C. Fuller, an early advocate of the use of armor in combat and planner of the major tank assault at Cambrai in late 1917, commented that Le Hamel stood alone among other battles of World War I in the rapidity, brevity, and thoroughness of its success. Australian historian Charles Bean commented that Le Hamel "furnished the model for almost every attack afterwards made by British infantry with tanks during the remainder of that war."

INTERWAR ACTIVITY

After World War I, the Mark V served extensively with White Russian forces during the Russian Civil War, as well as with British troops during their campaign in northern Russia. Active with the Soviet Red Army until the 1930s, the Mark V was reported to have been in service as late as 1941, and an example, long previously captured, was even said to have been used by the Germans as a fixed fortification during the defense of Berlin in 1945.

Two notable variants of the Mark V were introduced late in the war. The Mark V* included a lengthened hull to facilitate the crossing of enemy trench lines, and the Mark V** included a more functional length-width ratio for the longer tank. Four hundred Mark V tanks, 200 each of the Male and Female variants, were produced, while nearly 600 Mark V* tanks were built and only 25 of the Mark V**.

PzKpfw IV

Developed in the mid-1930s, the Panzerkampfwagen IV went on to become the stalwart of the German armored forces of World War II. The design holds the distinction of being the only German tank in continuous production throughout the war.

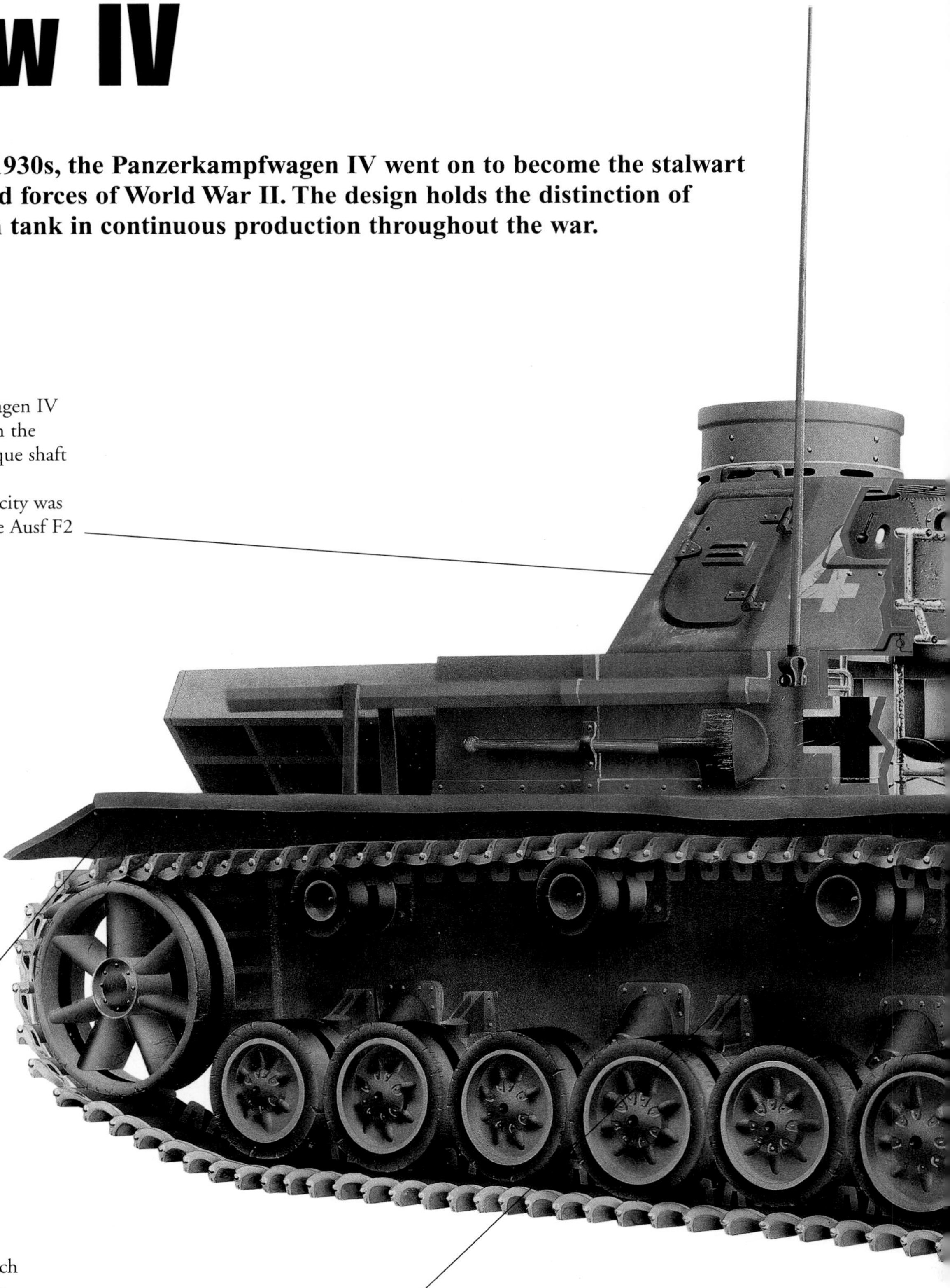

ASYMMETRICAL CONSTRUCTION
The turret of the Panzerkampfwagen IV was offset 2.6 in (66.5 mm) from the tank's centerline to allow the torque shaft to clear the rotary base junction. Therefore, the main storage capacity was on the right side of the tank. The Ausf F2 variant is shown here.

ENGINE
The Panzerkampfwagen IV was powered by a 12-cylinder Maybach HL 120 TRM engine, generating 296 hp (220 kW) and a top road speed of 26 mph (42 km/h).

SUSPENSION
A double bogey leaf spring suspension was installed on the Panzerkampfwagen IV chassis, replacing the preferred torsion bar suspension due to time limitations for the production of a new tank.

MAIN ARMAMENT
Although the initial Panzerkampfwagen IV Ausf F was equipped with the standard 2.95-in (75-mm) L/24 cannon, the Ausf F2, shown here, mounted the longer-barrelled 2.95-in (75-mm) L/43. The change significantly increased the weapon's muzzle velocity and its ability to penetrate the armor of Allied tanks.

FACTS

- More than 8500 of the PzKpfw IV were produced from 1936–45.

- The Syrian army deployed the PzKpfw IV during the 1967 Six-Day War.

- During 1943–44, PzKpfw IV production peaked with more than 6000 rolling off of the factory floors.

MOBILITY
Wider tracks, along with a modified front sprocket and rear idler wheel, improved the handling of the Panzerkampfwagen IV in difficult terrain. Ice sprags were fitted for winter weather.

RADIO OPERATOR'S POSITION
The radio operator, seated in the forward section on the right side, doubled as the hull machine gunner, firing a 0.31-in (7.92-mm) MG 34.

Initially designed as an infantry support medium tank to work in conjunction with the PzKpfw III, which was intended to engage enemy tanks, the PzKpfw IV was later fitted with more armor and guns to enable it to take over the tank fighting role.

PZKPFW IV AUSF F2 – SPECIFICATION

Country of Origin: Germany
Crew: 5
Designer: Krupp
Designed: 1936
In Service: 1939–67 (all Panzer IVs)
Manufacturer: Krupp, Steyr-Daimler-Puch
Number Built: 8800 (estimated, total Panzer IVs)
Produced: 1936–45
Gross Weight: 24.3 tons (22 tonnes)

Dimensions:
Hull Length: 19.4 ft (5.91 m)
Length (gun forward): 23 ft (7.02 m)
Width: 9.45 ft (2.88 m)
Overall Height: 8.8 ft (2.68 m)

Performance:
Maximum Speed: 26 mph (42 km/h)
Range, Road: 150 miles (240 km)
Range, Cross-country: 75 miles (120 km)
Power/Weight Ratio: 10.6 bhp/ton
Ground Pressure: 0.89 kg/cm²
Fording Capacity: 2.6ft (0.8m)
Maximum Gradient: 29 degrees
Maximum Trench Width: 7.55 ft (2.3 m)
Maximum Vertical Obstacle: 2.0 ft (0.6 m)
Suspension Type: Leaf spring

Engine:
Powerplant: Maybach HL120 12-cylinder in-line water-cooled gasoline engine
Transmission: 6 forward, 1 reverse speed
Capacity: 2.6 gallons (11.9 l)

Output: 296 hp (220 kW) @ 3000 rpm
Fuel Capacity: 103.5 gallons (470 l)

Armor & Armament:
Armor Type: Homogeneous rolled/welded nickel-steel
Hull Front: 2.36 in (60 mm)
Hull Sides: 1.18 in (30 mm)
Hull Rear: 0.78 in (20 mm)
Hull Top: 0.34 in (10 mm)
Hull Bottom: 0.34 in (10 mm)
Turret Front: 1.97 in (50 mm)
Turret Sides: 1.18 in (30 mm)
Turret Rear: 1.18 in (30 mm)
Turret Top: 0.59–0.98 in (15–25 mm)
Main: 1 x 2.95-in (75-mm) L/43 or L/48 KwK 40. 87 rounds
Secondary: 2 x 0.31-in (7.92-mm) MG34 MG. 3150 rounds

Panzer IV Numbers produced:

Date	Number of Vehicles	Variant
1937–39	262	Ausf A–D
1940	386	Ausf E
1941	769	
1942	880	Ausf E–G
1943	3013	Ausf H
1944	3125	Ausf J
1945	est. 435	

PZKPFW IV AUSF F1

In March 1941, production of the PzKpfw IV Ausf F, with increased hull, turret, and chassis armor, began. The weight of the Ausf F increased to 24.3 tons (22 tonnes), and its tracks were widened. The main Ausf F weapon was initially the same 2.95-in (75-mm) L/24 cannon of the earlier Ausf E. However, the F version was soon rearmed with the long-barrelled 2.95–in (75-mm) L/43 cannon. The L/24 version was designated F1, while those mounting the L/43 were designated F2. By June 1942, all PzKpfw IV tanks mounting the long-barrelled L/43 were reclassified as the Ausf G.

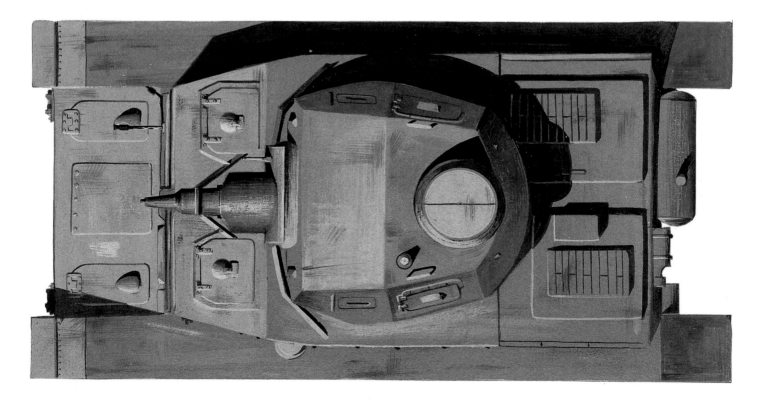

The PzKpfw IV was a mainstay of the German armored forces in World War II, and open ground proved to be ideal for such tanks. Here, German tanks advance on a broad front through waist-high winter wheat.

The Panzerkampfwagen IV, the workhorse of the German tank corps, was the most widely manufactured and deployed German tank of World War II. It was used as the base for many other fighting vehicles, including tank destroyers and self-propelled anti-aircraft guns.

The Panzerkampfwagen IV served in every theater of battle where German land forces were engaged during World War II. In continuous production – which began in 1936 and continued until the end of the war – more than 8500 Pzkpfw IV tanks were constructed, and the basic design was the only German tank that was in production throughout the duration of the conflict.

Conceived as an infantry support weapon, while the concurrently developed PzKpfw III was intended to engage enemy armored units, the PzKpfw IV was developed following specifications issued in January 1934 with a short-barrelled 2.96-in (75-mm) cannon and a pair of 0.31-in (7.92-mm) MG 34 machine guns. The new tank housed a crew of five, including a commander, gunner, loader, driver, and radio operator/forward machine gunner. While the PzKpfw III was initially armed with a 1.4-in (37-mm) main

gun, the heavier weapon on the PzKpfw IV was intended to deal with fixed fortifications, gun emplacements, and enemy troop concentrations that might impede the progress of German troops. General Heinz Guderian (a foremost proponent of the Blitzkrieg tactics that won Germany swift territorial gains in the early months of World War II) put forward the notion of a heavier medium tank.

RAPID SUCCESSION

The PzKpfw Ausf A entered service in 1936, and less than a year later a few B variants were produced with improvements to the engines and transmissions. By 1938, the PzKpfw Ausf C increased the turret armor to 1.18 in (30 mm). Nearly 500 of the F variant were produced starting in April 1941 and continuing to March 1942 as the role of the PzKpfw IV evolved to that of both a main battle tank and an infantry support weapon.

The Ausf F improved upon the E variant with several design alterations, including up to 2.36 in (60 mm) of hull armor and 1.96 in (50 mm) of armor protection in the turret, a ball-mounted hull machine gun, and wider tracks. The most significant modification to the Ausf F was in its main armament. The original F variant included the short-barrelled 2.96-in (75-mm) L/24 cannon. However, the high velocity, long-barrelled 2.96-in (75-mm) L/43 cannon was subsequently installed in numerous tanks, leading to the redesignation of the original as Ausf F1 and the latter as F2.

CONSTRUCTED AT SPEED

The upgunned F2 proved more than a match for British and American tanks in North Africa, but it was in short supply there. In the East, the F2 was, for a time, the mightiest tank in the German arsenal that was available in any numbers.

Later versions of the PzKpfw IV were heavily engaged on the Western Front but sustained serious losses at Falaise and during the Battle of the Bulge.

The last version of the tank, the PzKpfw IV Ausf J, was deployed in the spring of 1944. Its simplified construction meant it could be built quickly to urgently replace battlefield losses, yet its chassis could still serve as a platform for tank destroyers and mobile anti-aircraft weapons. Germany exported several hundred PzKpfw IVs to their Axis partners and other countries, and many of these remained in service long after the end of World War II.

Interior view

Manufactured in great numbers, the functional layout of the PzKpfw IV included space for both gunner and loader in the turret, on either side of the 2.96-in (75-mm) gun breech.

(1) **Turret Interior:** This was largely occupied by the operating system of the tank's heavy 2.95-in (75-mm) cannon.

(2) **Ammunition Racks:** These provided a ready supply of shells within the turret. Additional supplies of ammunition were stored in the hull of the PzKpfw IV.

(3) **Gun Cradle:** This provided a degree of stability for laying and firing the weapon, as well as support while the vehicle itself was in motion.

(4) **Breech Block:** The breech block of the turret-mounted 2.95-in (75-mm) cannon is shown. Early PzKpfw IV variants were armed with the short-barrelled L/24 cannon.

(5) **Machine Gun:** A turret-mounted 0.31-in (7.62-mm) machine gun was positioned to the right of the breech of the main weapon and fired through the turret mantlet.

(6) **Electrical Conduit:** The turret of the PzKpfw IV was capable of 360° traverse. This was accomplished primarily through electricity.

T-34/85

The most influential and successful tank of World War II, the T-34 combined elements of Soviet and Western design. It was produced in overwhelming numbers, becoming symbolic of the Red Army's victory on the Eastern Front.

MAIN ARMAMENT
Initially armed with the L-11 3-in (76.2-mm) cannon, the T-34 was upgunned to the long-barrelled F-34 3-in (76.2-mm) weapon, then to the more powerful ZiS-S-53 3.35-in (85-mm) cannon (shown) to keep pace with heavier German weaponry.

DRIVER
The sole occupant of the forward hull compartment, the driver of the T-34/85 was forced to function in limited space. Visibility was improved in later versions.

ROAD WHEELS
Early T-34 models were equipped with rubber road wheels. However, shortages of the material resulted in the adoption of steel rims.

FACTS

- The T-34 was developed from the BT series of fast tanks.

- In early 1944, the improved T-34/85 was introduced with a more powerful 3.35-in (85-mm) gun and a three-man turret design.

- Over 84,000 were built between 1944–58.

CUPOLA
Beginning in 1942, improvements to the T-34 included the addition of a commander's cupola for an improved field of vision.

TURRET
The original T-34 turret was cramped and accommodated only two crewmen. Later versions included a hexagonal configuration, and then a more spacious three-crew compartment.

RADIO
The radio of the T-34/85 was moved from the hull to the turret for better functionality. Initially, only the tanks of commanders were equipped with a radio.

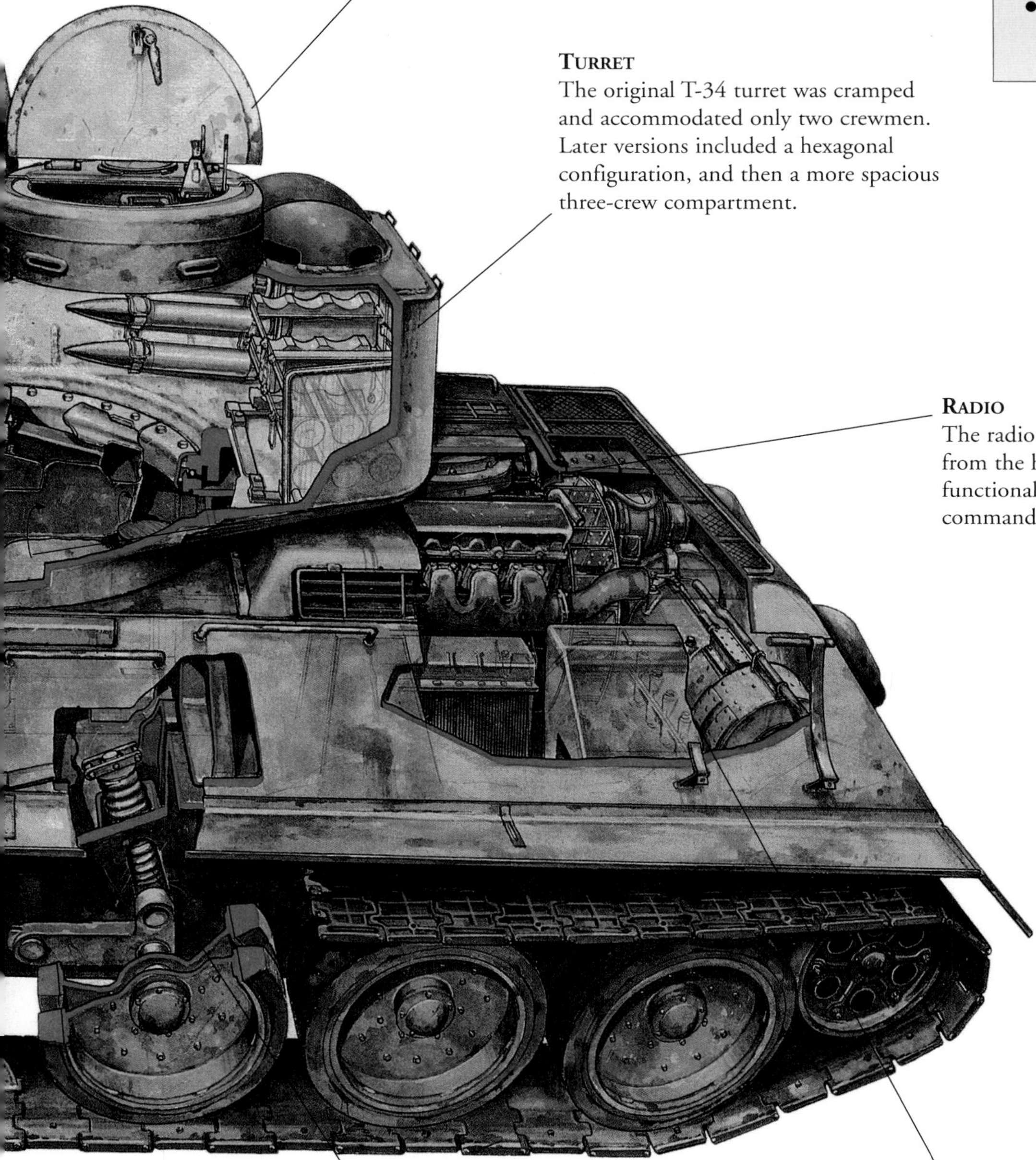

SUSPENSION
The T-34 incorporated a coil spring suspension developed by American engineer Walter Christie and first used in the earlier BT tank series.

ENGINE
The 12-cylinder V-2 diesel engine of the T-34 generated 500 hp (375 kW). Shortages of the engine resulted in the first production run being equipped with the MT-17 gas engine.

The tank's effectiveness in the battlefield suffered from the unsatisfactory ergonomic layout of its crew compartment. The two-man turret meant the commander also had to serve as gunner. Three-crew turrets, which accommodated a commander, gunner, and loader, proved superior.

T-34/85 – SPECIFICATION

Country of Origin: USSR
Crew: 5
Designer: Kharkiv Morozov Machine Building Design Bureau
Designed: 1937–40
In Service: 1940–present
Manufacturers: Various
Number Built: 84,070
Produced: 1940–58
Gross Weight: 35.2 tons (32 tonnes)

Dimensions:
Hull Length: 19.7 ft (6 m)
Length (gun forward): 24.6 ft (7.5 m)
Width: 9.6 ft (2.92 m)
Overall Height: 7.85 ft (2.39 m)

Performance:
Maximum Speed: 34 mph (55 km/h)
Range, Road: 188 miles (300 km)
Range, Cross-country: 100 miles (160 km)
Power/Weight Ratio: 16 bhp/ton
Ground Pressure: 0.087 kg/cm²
Fording Capacity: 3.3 ft (0.9 m)
Maximum Gradient: 30 degrees
Maximum Trench Width: 8.2 ft (2.5 m)
Max Vertical Obstacle: 2.6 ft (0.8 m)
Suspension: Trailing arm/coil spring

Engine:
Powerplant: 1 x V-2-34 V-12 water-cooled diesel engine

Capacity: 8.5 gallons (38.9 l)
Output: 500 bhp (375 kW) @ 2000 rpm
Fuel Capacity: 140 gallons (635 l)

Armor and Armaments:
Armor Type: Homogeneous rolled/welded nickel-steel
Hull Front: 1.8 in (45 mm)
Hull Sides: 1.8 in (45 mm)
Hull Rear: 1.6–1.8 in (40–45 mm)
Hull Top: 1.2 in (30 mm)
Hull Bottom: 0.8 in (20 mm)
Turret Front: 1.8–2.2 in (45–55 mm)
Turret Sides: 2–2.2 in (50–55 mm)
Turret Rear: 2 in (50 mm)
Turret Top: 0.8 in (20 m)
Main Armament: 3.35-in (85-mm) ZiS-S-53 cannon
Secondary Armament: 2 x 0.3-in (7.62-mm) MG34 machine guns

Operators:
USSR
Albania
Austria
Bulgaria
Cyprus
Czechoslovakia
Cuba
Finland
East Germany
Hungary
Poland
Romania
Yugoslavia
Afghanistan
Egypt
Indonesia
Iraq
Laos
Lebanon
Libya
Mongolia
North Korea
Palestine (12 operated by the PLO in Lebanon, passed on to the Al-Murabitun)
People's Republic of China
Syria
Vietnam
South Yemen (PDRY)
North Yemen (YAR)
Algeria
Angola
Republic of the Congo
Equatorial Guinea
Ethiopia
Guinea
Guinea-Bissau
Mali
Mozambique
Somalia
Sudan
Togo
Zimbabwe

T-34/85

The T-34/85 improved the original T-34 design with a three-man turret compartment. This enabled the commander to direct the tank in combat more efficiently, relieving him of the requirement to serve the main cannon. It also incorporated a heavier 3.35-in (85-mm) main weapon, which was capable of penetrating the armor of the wartime generation of German tanks at moderate distances. Early T-34s, based on the BT series originally conceived by American engineer Walter Christie (1865–1944), introduced sloped armor but were limited in their combat effectiveness because of the poor layout of the crew compartment and the installation of radios only in commanders' tanks, which hampered communications.

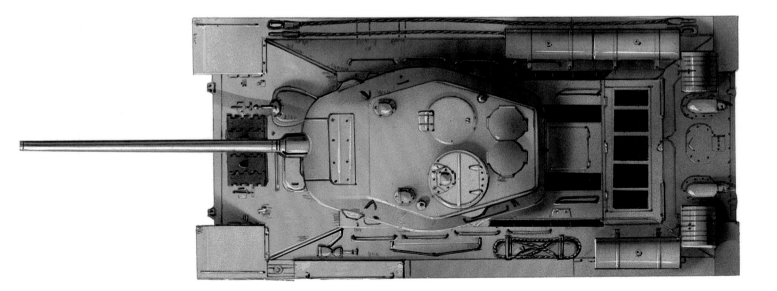

A column of T-34 tanks halts along a snowy road on the Eastern Front as Red Army soldiers clamber aboard during the advance towards the German frontier in the winter of 1944.

The T-34/85 of early 1944 gave the Red Army a tank with better armor and mobility than the German PzKpfw IV and Sturmgeschütz III, but it could not match the Panther in gun or armor protection. However, the T-34/85 was good enough to allow skilled crews to tip the balance.

General Heinz Guderian's Panzergruppe II met the Red Army's T-34 medium tank in combat for the first time in November 1941. At that point, it became readily apparent that German armored forces were confronting a Soviet tank capable of holding its own ferociously on the battlefield.

"Numerous Russian T-34s went into action and inflicted heavy losses on the German tanks at Mzensk in 1941," wrote Guderian after the war. "Up to this time we had enjoyed tank superiority, but from now on the situation was reversed. The prospect of rapid decisive victories was fading in consequence. I made a report on this situation, which for us was a new one, and sent it to the Army Group. In this report, I described in plain terms the marked superiority of the T-34 to our PzKpfw IV and drew the relevant conclusion as that must affect our future tank production."

Although the appearance of the T-34 came as a shock to the Germans, the tank itself had been in design since the mid-1930s, and the prototype for the new Soviet medium

battle tank, replacing the earlier BT series and T-26 vehicles, had been developed by 1940. The combination of rapid mobility, increasingly effective firepower, sloping armor, and deployment in large numbers established the T-34 as the pivotal weapon on the Eastern Front during World War II.

DARING DESIGN

From the beginning, the T-34 was a platform for innovation. It could reach a top road speed of 34 mph (55 km/h) powered by its 12-cylinder V-2 engine. Its sloped armor, on average 2 in (52 mm) thick, provided greater protection against enemy fire through increased thickness without added weight. More often, incoming shells tended to deflect. However, early versions of the T-34 were hampered by the requirement that the commander serve the main 3-in (76.2-mm) cannon. In addition, communications were limited because radios were only installed in commanders' tanks.

By the spring of 1944, the T-34/85 had incorporated numerous design improvements, among them the addition of the ZiS-S-53 3.35-in (85-mm) cannon, which was effective against German armor at moderate distances, and a larger three-man turret, which could accommodate a loader and gunner to service the main weapon. More than 57,000 T-34 variants were constructed throughout World War II, an astonishing feat considering that the bulk of Soviet industrial production had been relocated to the east of the Ural Mountains following the German invasion of the Soviet Union on June 22, 1941. A total of 22,500 T-34/85 tanks were constructed, and during the course of the war production time was cut in half while unit cost was substantially reduced as well.

STAGGERING LOSSES REPLACED

In combat, the performance of the T-34 suffered because crews lacked thorough training, and their battlefield tactics evolved only slowly. To nullify the advantage of 2.95-in (75-mm) and 3.5-in (88-mm) weapons on the German heavy tanks, which were capable of destroying a T-34 at a distance of more than 1 mile (1.6 km), the Soviets attempted to close rapidly with the enemy, charging en masse and often without coordination. Losses were staggering, yet Soviet factories were more than able to compensate. Ultimately, the T-34 stood up to the costly and over-engineered German tanks, which were available only in limited numbers.

World War II variants of the T-34 included self-propelled assault guns, a flamethrower version, and recovery and bridging tanks. Improvements continued into the 1960s, and examples of the tank remain in service to this day.

Interior view

The interior of the early T-34 medium tank was not built with comfort in mind. Primitive by Western standards, the design underwent steady improvement during and after World War II.

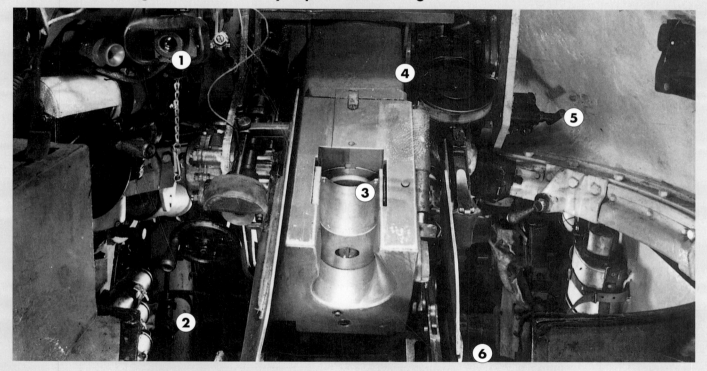

1. **Gun Laying Equipment:** The main 3.35-in (85-mm) cannon of the T-34/85 tank was sighted with optical tools from inside the turret and adjacent to the weapon itself.

2. **Turret Traverse Mechanism:** The turret was traversed electrically, distinguished by a slight bulge in the turret.

3. **Breech Block:** The upgunned T-34/85 mounted the powerful ZiS-S-53 3.34-in (85-mm) cannon, which was capable of penetrating most German armor.

4. **Gun Cradle:** The cradle of the ZiS-S-53 3.35-in (85-mm) cannon supported the weapon during operation and absorbed some of the recoil of the powerful weapon.

5. **Turret Armor:** The turret was cast to up to 2.95 in (75 mm) thick on the front and sides and 0.78 in (20 mm) on its roof.

6. **Turret Floor:** The lack of a rotating turret basket on which the gunner and loader could stand during combat hampered the T-34/85.

M4A4 Sherman

Developed, manufactured, and deployed at great speed, the ubiquitous Medium Tank M4, popularly known as the Sherman, was produced in great numbers. Successfully countering the heavier armor and armament of contemporary German armored fighting vehicles, the M4 became a symbol of Allied victory.

SILHOUETTE
The high silhouette of the M4 Sherman was protected against direct fire by sloped armor, but its distinct profile presented an inviting target in open country.

ENGINE
While its powerplant was changed in variants, the M4A4 was powered by the 425-hp (317-kW), five-bank Chrysler A57 engine.

SECONDARY ARMAMENT
The M4 was armed with a turret-mounted 0.5-in (12.7-mm) Browning machine gun for anti-aircraft defense, and a 0.3-in (7.62-mm) Browning M1919A4 mounted coaxially in the turret. A second 0.3-in (7.62-mm) faced forwards in the hull.

FACTS

- Nearly 50,000 Medium Tank M4 variants were produced between 1941–45.

- The M4 was the most numerous tank in service with the British Army during World War II.

- The M4 design remained in service with some armed forces into the 1970s.

MAIN ARMAMENT
The Medium Tank M4 was originally armed with a 2.95-in (75-mm) M3 L/40 cannon, as depicted in the M4A4. Other variants were armed with a 3-in (76-mm) cannon, a 4-in (105-mm) howitzer, and the British QF 17-pounder anti-tank gun.

AMMUNITION STORAGE
The M4 allowed for wet storage of up to 90 rounds of 2.95-in (75-mm) ammunition, reducing the risk of explosion.

CREW
The crew of the M4 Sherman included a commander, ammunition loader, gunner, driver, and an assistant driver who doubled as a machine gunner. The driver was positioned left and forwards, operating two steering levers and foot pedals.

ARMOR PROTECTION
The M4A4 Sherman's armor protection ranged in thickness from 0.78–3.34 in (20 to 85 mm) in more vulnerable areas.

The M4 was renowned as "the tank that won World War II." The aim of its existence had been to build a tank to correct many of the deficiencies of the M3 mediums but still use as many of the components of the M3 as possible.

M4A4 SHERMAN – SPECIFICATION

Country of Origin: USA
Crew: 5
Designer: U.S. Army Ordnance Department
Designed: 1940
Manufacturer: Detroit Tank Arsenal (Chrysler)
In Production: 1941–50s
In Service: 1942–55
Number Produced: 50,000+
Gross Weight: 34.8 tons (31.62 tonnes)

Dimensions:
Hull Length: 19.8 ft (6.06 m)
Length (gun forward): 19.8 ft (6.06 m)
Width: 9.5 ft (2.9 m)
Overall Height: 9.33 ft (2.84 m)

Performance:
Maximum Speed: 29 mph (47 km/h)
Range, Road: 100 miles (160 km)
Range, Cross-country: 60 miles (100 km)
Ground Pressure: 0.92 kg/cm²
Fording Capacity: 3.5 ft (1.1 m)
Maximum Gradient: 30 degrees
Maximum Trench Width: 8 ft (2.44 m)
Maximum Vertical Obstacle: 2 ft (0.6 m)
Suspension Type: Vertical volute sprung two-wheel bogies

Engine:
Powerplant: 1 x Chrysler A57 30 cylinder multibank gas engine
Capacity: 4.5 gallons (20.5 l)
Output: 425 hp (317 kW) @ 2850 rpm
Power/Weight Ratio: 12.2 bhp/ton
Fuel Capacity: 133.3 gallons (605 l)

Armament and Armor:
Main Armament: 1 x 2.95-in (75-mm) M3 L/40 in M4A4 Mount
Secondary Armament: 2 x 0.3-in (7.62-mm) M1919A4 Browning MG
Ancillary Armament: 0.5-in (12.7-mm) M2HB MG in AA mount
Armor Type: Homogeneous rolled/welded; cast hull, cast turret
Hull Front: 2 in (50 mm)
Hull Sides: 1.5 in (38 mm)
Hull Rear: 1.5 in (38 mm)
Hull Top: 0.75 in (9 mm)
Hull Bottom: 0.5–1 in (12.5–25 mm)
Turret Front: 2–3.3 in (50–85 mm)
Turret Sides: 2 in (50 mm)
Turret Rear: 2 in (50 mm)
Turret Top: 1 in (25 mm)

Variants:
3-in (76.2-mm) Gun Motor Carriage M10: Tank Destroyer.
3.54-in (90-mm) Gun Motor Carriage M36: Tank Destroyer.
4-in (105-mm) Howitzer Motor Carriage M7: Self-propelled artillery (Priest).
6-in (155-mm) Gun Motor Carriage M12: GMC M12 with Cargo Carrier M30.
Flame Tank Sherman: M4A3R3 Zippo, M4 Crocodile, and other flame-throwing Shermans.
Rocket Artillery Sherman: T34 Calliope, T40 Whizbang, and other Sherman rocket launchers.
Amphibious tanks: Duplex Drive (DD) swimming Sherman.
Engineer tanks: Including D-8, M1, and M1A1 dozers, M4 Doozit, Mobile Assault Bridge, and Aunt Jemima.
Recovery tanks: M32 and M74 TRVs.
Artillery tractors: M34 and M35 prime movers.

M4A4 SHERMAN FIREFLY

A multitude of Medium Tank M4 variants were produced during World War II. The distinguishing features of the M4A4 were its Chrysler A57 engine and the modifications to its hull that enabled the tank to accommodate its increased size. The 30-cylinder, five-bank 425-hp (317-kW) Chrysler A57 was introduced on the M4A4 to increase its power. In turn, the welded upper hull, which was used in all Shermans, was lengthened 11 in (28 cm) over other variants. The road wheels on the M4A4 were spaced about 10 in (25 cm) apart, considerably more than the 3.5 in (9 cm) seen on other models. The variant shown here is the M4A4 Sherman Firefly with a 0.3-in (7.62-mm) gun.

Illustrating the sheer weight of numbers that tipped the balance of armored warfare in favor of the Allies during World War II, a formation of M4A4 Sherman tanks are seen here coming to a halt in the desert.

The Sherman proved to be an excellent fighting platform and went on to be constructed in the thousands. It suffered a wide range of drawbacks but, ultimately, the numerical superiority of the M4 made it a war winner.

An icon of the Allied victory in World War II, the Medium Tank M4, nicknamed Sherman by the British who used it in large numbers through Lend Lease, was built in greater quantity than any other Allied tank except the Soviet T-34. Even as its predecessor, the M3, was on American assembly lines and deploying to the battlefields of North Africa, the M4 was hurriedly being developed. By September 1941, the prototype, designated T6, was completed.

The Sherman made its combat debut with British forces during the pivotal Battle of El Alamein in October 1942 and easily withstood the onslaughts of earlier German armor, like the PzKpfw III and IV. However, with the introduction of the heavier Panther and Tiger tanks, the pronounced shortcomings of the Sherman became apparent. Its main gun, the 2.95-in (75-mm) M3 L/40, was woefully inadequate against the heavy armor of the later German tanks, while the

high-velocity German guns were capable of penetrating the Sherman's armor at distances of a mile (1.6 km) or more.

STRENGTH IN NUMBERS

In combat, a platoon of four Shermans would often be required to take on a single Tiger tank, and losses were a virtual certainty. However, the might of American industry, which churned out nearly 50,000 Shermans through numerous manufacturers during the war years, made good on the heavy losses. This enabled the Allied Shermans to overwhelm their enemy numerically. If the Sherman had a tactical advantage, it was its maximum road speed of 29 mph (47 km/h) and maneuverability.

The primary variants of the M4 included the M4A1, M4A2, M4A3, and M4A4, distinguished mainly by their varying powerplants. Some later models were equipped with a larger turret and a high-velocity 3-in (76-mm) gun. The British substituted the QF 17-pounder anti-tank gun on top of the M4A4 chassis to create a more powerful variant called the Firefly. Some M4s were also upgunned with a 4-in (105-mm) howitzer. The various designations did not necessarily indicate improvements over time, but often modifications in concurrent production models.

The M4A4 hull was lengthened to accommodate its Chrysler A57 engine. Other engines included the 353-hp (263-kW) Wright Whirlwind, 400-hp (298-kW) Continental R975, 450-hp (335-kW) Caterpillar 9-cylinder diesel, 420-hp (313-kW) General Motors 6-71 diesel, and 500-hp (372-kW) Ford GAA III. The M4A1 hull was fully cast, and not simply a combination of cast and welded construction, while the vertical volute spring suspension was replaced with a horizontal configuration on the M4A3.

During World War II, the M4 chassis was modified to perform a number of functions, such as a flail tank for clearing mines, rocket launcher, ammunition carrier, bulldozer, recovery vehicle, and flamethrower. Perhaps the most famous of these variants was the DD (Duplex Drive) tank. This had a canvas screen for flotation and was intended to provide fire support for Allied troops directly on the invasion beaches during the D-Day landings on June 6, 1944. The Sherman was also deployed in the Pacific and outclassed any armor the Japanese fielded.

The Medium Tank M4 Sherman was arguably one of the most significant weapons of World War II. Despite its shortcomings, it enabled the Allies to win the war.

Interior view

The M4A4 Sherman tank was fast and maneuverable, though its armor protection was inadequate against high-caliber German shells. Its interior was functional but felt compact with a crew of five.

(1) Electrical Circuitry: Internally, the M4A4 Sherman relied largely on electricity in order to function.

(2) Ammunition Storage: High-explosive and armor-piercing shells were stored near the 2.95-in (75-mm) cannon and also in "wet" storage areas within the hull.

(3) Mesh Screen: Operational areas within the M4A4 Sherman were separated by mesh screens. This avoided obstruction during combat but allowed efficient communication.

(4) Air Cleaner: An air-cleaning apparatus was connected to the engine and located at the rear of the crew compartment.

(5) Engine Access: The 425-hp (317-kW) five-bank Chrysler A57 engine produced a maximum road speed of 29 mph (47 km/h).

(6) Crew Compartment: The five-man crew of the M4A4 Sherman tank included three in the turret and crew compartment with a driver and assistant driver/machine gunner forwards in the hull.

PzKpfw V Panther

The capture of a Soviet T-34 medium tank on the Eastern Front led directly to the development of the German Panzerkampfwagen V Panther, which incorporated a number of the design elements of the T-34 and became an exceptional armored weapon in its own right.

MAIN ARMAMENT
The primary weapon mounted by the Panzerkampfwagen V Panther was the 2.95-in (75-mm) KwK 42 L/70 high-velocity cannon manufactured by Rheinmetall-Borsig.

ARMOR PROTECTION
The Panther's frontal armor was up to 3.2 in (80 mm) thick. Its 55-degree slope effectively increased the protection afforded the five-man crew. Side armor, which varied from 1.6 in (40 mm) to 2 in (50 mm), could be considered a defensive weakness.

AMMUNITION STORAGE
No ammunition was stored in the Panther's turret. However, up to 48 rounds of 2.95-in (75-mm) ammunition were carried in sponsons on either side of the hull.

TURRET
The Panther tank incorporated an existing three-man turret design that underwent several modifications. Later versions included a cast commander's cupola rather than an early drum-like configuration and a bracket for an MG 34 anti-aircraft machine gun.

FACTS

- The high-velocity 2.95-in (75-mm) cannon gave the Panther a main armament that was initially superior to most Allied guns.
- Daimler-Benz and Maschinenfabrik Augsburg-Nürnberg AG (MAN) competed for the contract to manufacture the Panther.
- The debut of the Panther at the Battle of Kursk was inauspicious because of mechanical failures.

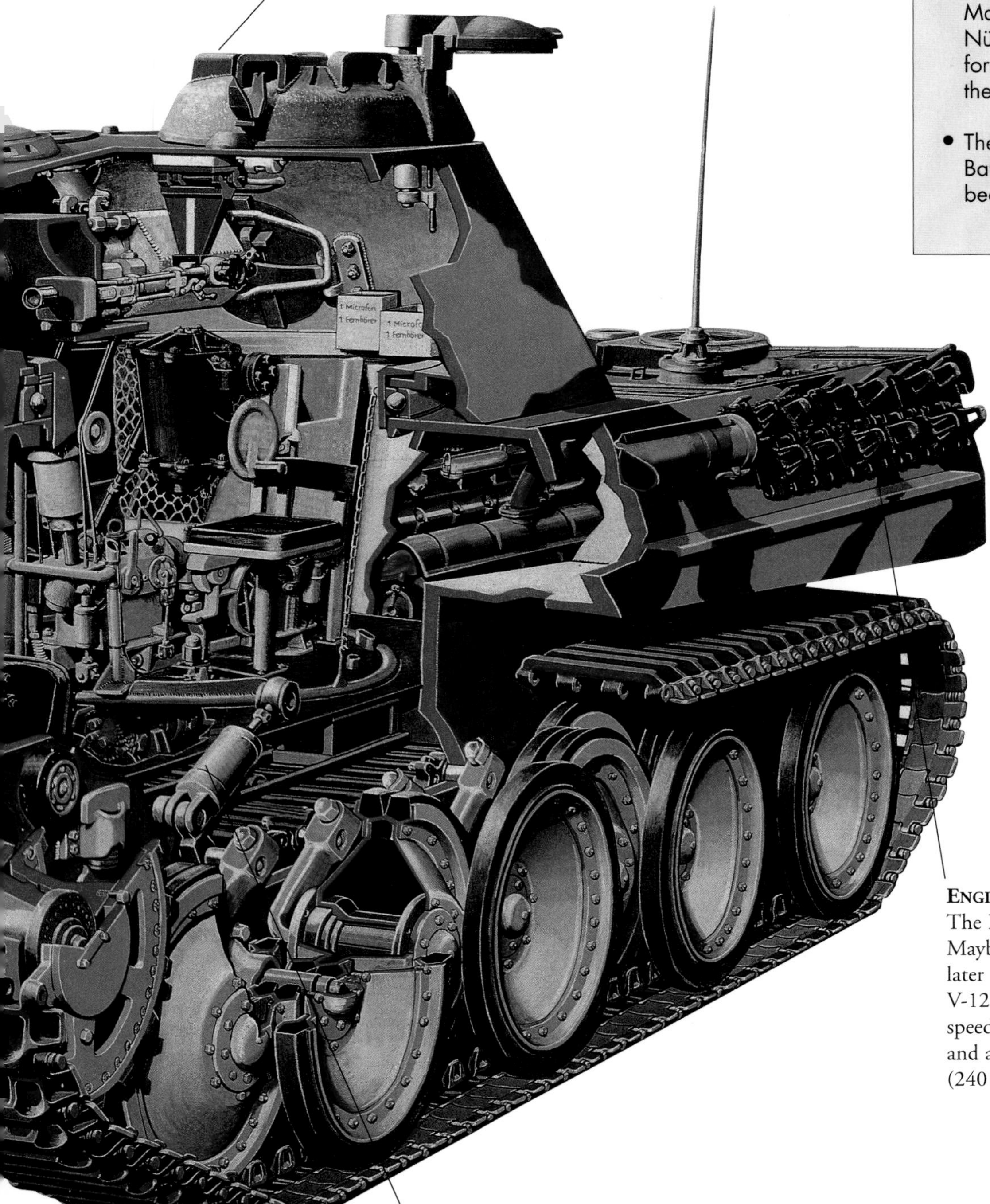

ENGINE
The Panther's 650-hp (485-kW) Maybach HL 210 P 45 gas engine was later improved to a 690-hp (514.5-kW) V-12 Maybach HL230 P30 with a top speed in excess of 30 mph (48 km/h) and a range of more than 150 miles (240 km).

SUSPENSION
The distinctive suspension of the Panther included a double torsion bar arrangement with interwoven road wheels. This allowed the vehicle to traverse difficult terrain more easily. Wide tracks offered greater stability.

The Panther was sent to frontline units in the spring of 1943 and first saw major combat at Kursk. With the correction of the production-related mechanical difficulties, the Panther became highly popular with German tankers and a fearsome weapon on the battlefield.

PZKPFW V PANTHER AUSF A – SPECIFICATION

Country of Origin: Germany
Crew: 5
Designer: MAN AG
Designed: 1942
In Service: 1943–45
Manufacturers: MAN, Daimler-Benz, Maschinenfabrik
    Niedersachsen-Hannover (MNH), Henschel & Sohn
Number Built: 6000
Produced: 1942–45
Gross Weight: 50.1 tons (45.5 tonnes)

Dimensions:
Hull Length: 22.6 ft (6.9 m)
Length (gun forward): 29 ft (8.86 m)
Width: 10.75 ft (3.27 m)
Width (with skirts): 11.25 ft (3.42 m)
Overall Height: 9.9 ft (3 m)

Performance:
Maximum Speed: 30 mph (48 km/h)
Range, Road: 120 miles (200 km)
Range, Cross-country: 60 miles (100 km)
Ground Pressure: 0.75 kg/cm²
Fording Capacity: 6.2 ft (1.9 m)
Maximum Gradient: 36 degrees
Maximum Trench Width: 8 ft (2.45 m)
Maximum Vertical Obstacle: 3 ft (0.9 m)
Suspension Type: Torsion bar

Engine:
Powerplant: 1 x Maybach HL230 P30 V-12 water-cooled
    gas engine
Capacity: 5 gallons (23 l)

Output: 690 hp (514.5 kW) @ 3000 rpm
Power/Weight Ratio: 15.5 bhp/ton
Fuel Capacity: 160.6 gallons (730 l)

Armor and Armament:
Armor Type: Homogenous rolled/welded nickel-steel
Hull Front: 2–3.2 in (50–80 mm)
Hull Sides: 1.6–2 in (40–50 mm)
Hull Rear: 1.6 in (40 mm)
Hull Top: 0.6 in (16 mm)
Hull Bottom: 0.6 in (16 mm)
Turret Front: 4 in (100 mm)
Turret Sides: 1.8 in (45 mm)
Turret Rear: 1.8 in (45 mm)
Turret Top: 0.6 in (16 mm)
Main Armament: 1 x 2.95-in (75-mm) KwK42 L/70.
    82 rounds.
Secondary Armament: 2 x 0.31-in (7.92-mm) MG34
    machine guns. 4800 rounds.
Ancillary Armament: 3.6-in (92-mm) bomb/grenade launcher

Derived Vehicles:
Jagdpanther: Heavy tank destroyer with the 3.45-in (88-mm)
    L/71 gun.
Befehlspanzer Panther: Command tank with additional radio
    equipment.
Beobachtungspanzer Panther: Observation tank for artillery
    spotters; dummy gun; armed with only two MG34.
Bergepanther: Armored recovery vehicle.

PZKPFW V PANTHER AUSF D

In the summer of 1942, the Panzerkampfwagen V medium tank, known popularly as the Panther, was rushed into production to counter the superiority of the Soviet-made T-34 on the Eastern Front. The Panther design included several elements of the T-34, such as sloping armor and wider road wheels. Incorporating an existing turret design, the Panther mounted a high-velocity 2.95-in (75-mm) L/70 cannon, which was capable of penetrating up to 6 in (150 mm) of armor at a distance of 3280 ft (1000 m). Unlike the cramped turret of the T-34, the Panther turret accommodated three crewmen and provided for better command and control in battle. The Ausf D variant is shown here.

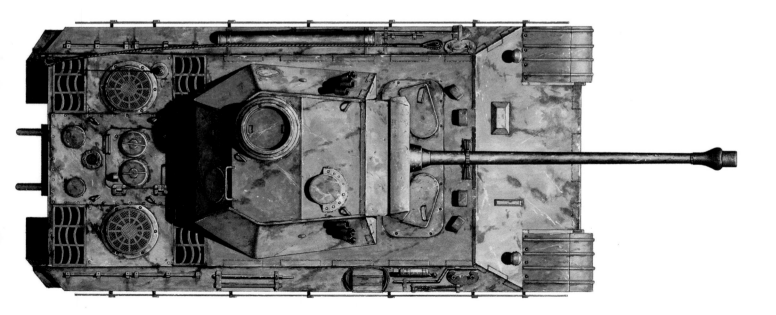

To destroy a Panther, a tank destroyer with a 3-in (76-mm) gun would have to aim for the side or rear of the turret (the opening through which the hull-mounted machine gun projected), or target the underside of the gun shield.

In one single day of combat in late July 1944, SS Oberscharführer (Technical Sergeant) Ernst Barkmann wrote the most famous chapter of his combat career on the Western Front. Near the French village of Le Lorey, Barkmann placed his Panther medium tank among a thick stand of oak trees and waited for an advancing Allied armored formation.

As a column of 15 American Sherman tanks came into view, the lone Panther quickly knocked out the two leading vehicles as well as a tanker truck attached to the column.

Interior view

The turret of the Panther tank was adapted from a previous design and improved in later variants. Its distinctively sloped armor is apparent from the interior, yet the space accommodated three crewmen.

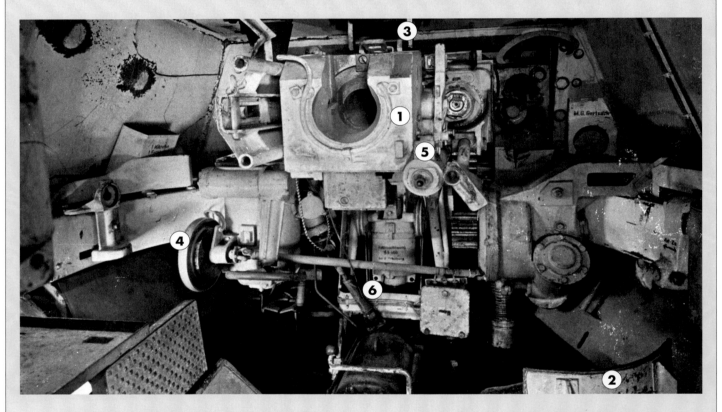

(1) **Breech Block:** The breech block of the 2.9-in (75-mm) cannon dominates this image of the turret interior. Its high muzzle velocity made an effective long-range weapon.

(2) **Loader's Seat:** The loader sat to the right of the breech block, able to supply 2.9-in (75-mm) ammunition easily within reach.

(3) **Turret Hatch:** Access to and from the Panther's turret was easily accomplished through a hatch mounted on the roof.

(4) **Traversing Gear:** The manual traversing gear was used to operate the turret of the PzKpfw V in the event of an electrical failure or damage sustained in battle.

(5) **Sighting and Recoil Equipment:** Recoil and sighting mechanisms were utilized to visually acquire a target.

(6) **Elevation Apparatus:** The Panther's 2.9-in (75-mm) L70 cannon was raised or lowered using powered or manual controls.

A column of Panther tanks rolls towards the front during bitter winter fighting. Early Panthers were plagued by mechanical and design flaws yet, ultimately, the PzKpfw V responded ferociously to the Soviet T-34.

Barkmann then hit and disabled two more Shermans attempting to skirt around the wreckage of the earlier victims. As the Americans regrouped, they called for tactical air support, and the Panther was damaged during the ensuing attack. Still, Barkmann defended his ground, knocking out two further Shermans as they closed in. Finally, he was able to coax his damaged tank to safety in the town of Neufbourg.

Against long odds, Barkmann had destroyed nine Sherman tanks and several support vehicles. For this and other exploits in combat, the leading Panther ace of the war received the Knight's Cross of the Iron Cross. He also further enhanced the reputation of the Panzerkampfwagen V Panther as a rugged and formidable foe.

Although the Panther earned a fearsome reputation, the swiftness of its development and deployment resulted in numerous mechanical failures, particularly during the Battle of Kursk. General Heinz Guderian, a famed panzer commander, further stated, "They burnt too easily, the fuel and oil systems were insufficiently protected, and the crews were lost due to lack of training."

RAPID MATURITY

Nevertheless, the Panther's superb long-barrelled 2.95-in (75-mm) cannon and its overall design fostered the development of the tank into one of the finest fighting vehicles of World War II. Following a design competition, which was fought principally between Daimler-Benz and Maschinenfabrik Augsburg Nürnberg (MAN), the MAN design was placed in production. In the summer of 1942, MAN produced two prototypes, and a small production run of only 20 tanks was supplanted by the Ausf D, approximately 250 of which entered service beginning in January 1943. It was this version that took part in the Battle of Kursk. A number of these broke down or were lost because of problems with the transmission or suspension and there were even engine compartment fires. A further 850 improved Ausf D models, with larger engines and redesigned turrets and armor skirts, were manufactured until September 1943.

AUSF G

Curiously designated Ausf A, another variant was placed in production in August 1943, and during the following 10 months more than 2100 were manufactured by MAN, Henschel, Daimler-Benz, and Demag. However, the greatest production version of the Panther was the Ausf G, which incorporated several improvements to the exhaust system, tapered armor on the upper hull, and a rotating driver's periscope. Starting in the spring of 1944 until the end of the war, production of the Ausf G neared 3000 tanks.

PzKpfw VI Tiger

Perhaps the most famous tank of World War II, the Tiger epitomized the German penchant for quality over quantity. Its engineering requirements and high cost precluded the Tiger from being produced in large numbers. However, the prowess of the Tiger on the battlefield was incontestable.

MAIN ARMAMENT
The formidable 3.5-in (88-mm) KwK 36 L/56 cannon, modified to fit the Tiger turret, had already proven itself in the anti-aircraft and anti-tank roles. Complemented with precision optics, its flat trajectory and range were deadly to enemy tanks.

ARMOR PROTECTION
The frontal hull and turret armor of the Tiger, at 4 in (100 mm) and 4.8 in (120 mm) respectively, were substantially thicker than those of the PzKpfw IV.

MOBILITY
The twin radius steering system, hydraulically controlled pre-selector gearbox, and semi-automatic transmission were state of the art but prone to mechanical difficulties.

SUSPENSION
The torsion bar suspension of the Tiger was divided equally with eight bars on each side, while its interwoven wheels proved problematic in the field.

FACTS

- Only 1347 Tigers were produced between 1942 and 1944, while lighter Allied tanks were manufactured in great quantity.
- Following a demonstration on Hitler's birthday, Henschel received the contract for the Tiger.
- The cost to build a Tiger was twice that of the PzKpfw IV.

TURRET
With a 360-degree circular floor, the turret of the Tiger tank weighed 11 tons (9.9 tonnes). The gunner sat to the left with the commander at his rear, and the loader occupying a folding seat.

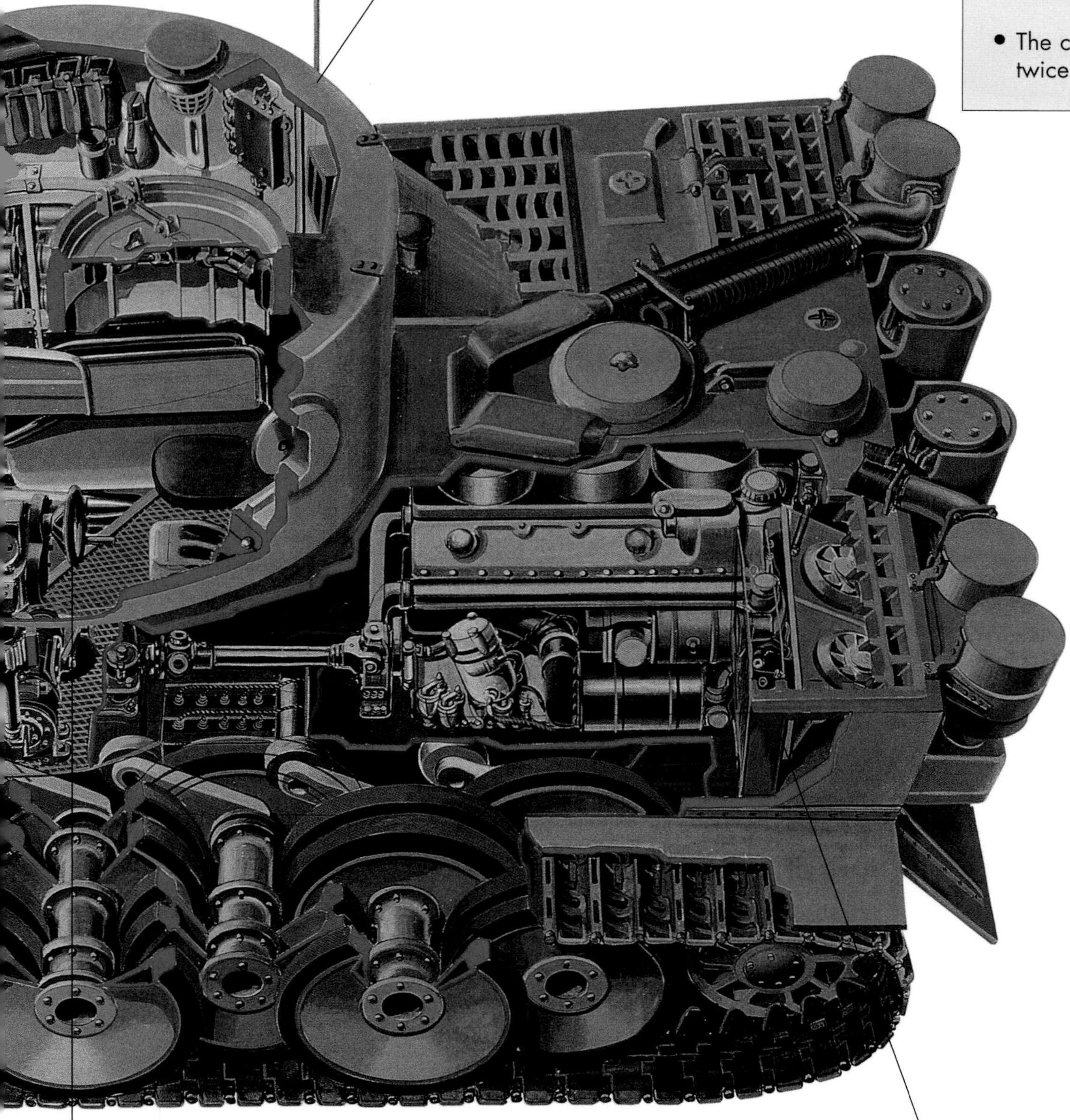

CREW COMPARTMENT
The driver and radio operator were situated to the left and right of the large gearbox respectively.

ENGINE
After 250 Tigers were produced, the original 642-hp (479-kW), 12-cylinder Maybach HL 210 P45 engine was deemed inadequate for the 57-ton (52-tonne) behemoth and replaced by the 690-hp (514.5-kW) V-12 HL 230 P45.

With five men in a very small area, the interior of the Tiger was somewhat dark and fairly cramped. In addition to that, the crewmen had to make room for at least 92 of the big gun's 3.5-in (88-mm) shells.

TIGER – SPECIFICATION

Country of Origin: Germany
Crew: 5
Designer: Henschel & Son
Designed: 1942
In Service: 1942–45
Manufacturer: Henschel
Number Built: 1347
Produced: 1942–44
Gross Weight: 57 tons (52 tonnes)

Dimensions:
Hull Length: 20.75 ft (6.32 m)
Length (gun forward): 27.75 ft (8.46 m)
Width: 12.25 ft (3.73 m)
Overall Height: 9.5 ft (2.9 m)

Performance:
Maximum Speed:
  Max speed 1st gear 1.8 mph (2.8 km/h)
  Max speed 2nd gear 2.7 mph (4.3 km/h)
  Max speed 3rd gear 3.8 mph (6.2 km/h)
  Max speed 4th gear 5.7 mph (9.2 km/h)
  Max speed 5th gear 8.7 mph (14.1 km/h)
  Max speed 6th gear 13 mph (20.9 km/h)
  Max speed 7th gear 18.9 mph (30.5 km/h)
  Max speed 8th gear 28 mph (45.4 km/h)
  Max speed 1st reverse gear 1.8 mph (2.8 km/h)
  Max speed 2nd reverse gear 2.7 mph (4.3 km/h)
  Max speed 3rd reverse gear 3.8 mph (6.2 km/h)
  Max speed 4th reverse gear 5.7 mph (9.2 km/h)
Range, Road: 120 miles (195 km)
Range, Cross-country: 65 miles (110 km)
Power/Weight Ratio: 12.3 bhp/ton

Ground Pressure: 0.074 kg/cm²
Fording Capacity: 3.3 ft (1.6 m)
Maximum Gradient: 36 degrees
Maximum Trench Width: 7.55 ft (2.3 m)
Maximum Vertical Obstacle: 2.6 ft (0.8 m)
Suspension Type: Torsion bar

Engine:
Powerplant: 1 x Maybach HL230P45 V-12 water-cooled gas engine
Capacity: 5.1 gallons (23 l)
Output: 642 bhp (479 kW) @ 3000 rpm
Fuel Capacity: 119 gallons (540 l)

Armor and Armament:
Armor Type: Homogeneous rolled/welded nickel-steel
Hull Front: 4 in (100 mm)
Hull Sides: 2.4–3.32 in (60–80 mm)
Hull Rear: 3.2 in (80 mm)
Hull Top: 1 in (25 mm)
Hull Bottom: 0.2 in (5 mm)
Turret Front: 4–4.8 in (100–120 mm)
Turret Sides: 3.2 in (80 mm)
Turret Rear: 3.2 in (80 mm)
Turret Top: 1 in (25 m)
Main Armament: 1 x 3.05-in (88-mm) KwK 36 L/56
Secondary Armament: 2 x 0.31-in (7.92-mm) MG34 machine guns
Ancillary Armament: Grenade/bomb launchers

TIGER

Both Henschel and Porsche submitted prototype designs for the Tiger, and in August 1942, Henschel began production of the 57-ton (52-tonne) tank. Although its capabilities as a fighting vehicle were readily apparent, the Tiger was placed in service following limited trials because of time constraints, while numerous design innovations made production slow and costly and created performance issues in the field. The Tiger's low clearance restricted maneuverability in rugged terrain, and its overlapping wheel configuration was difficult to maintain and prone to break down because of icing, heavy mud, or rocks lodging between components. The tank's heavy weight made it a tremendous task to transport it by rail or to tow and recover a damaged Tiger.

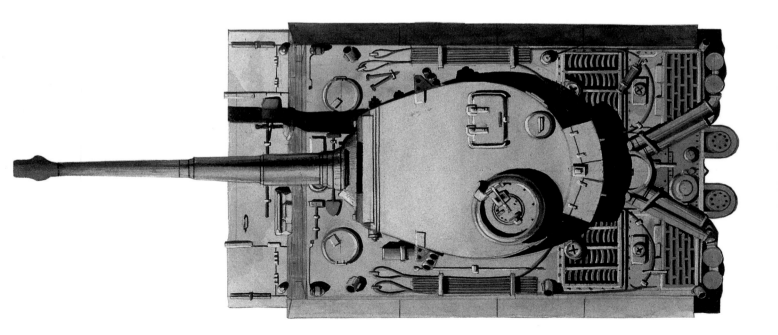

"I had no time to assemble my company; instead I had to act quickly, as I had to assume that the enemy had already spotted me. I set off with one tank and passed the order to the others not to retreat."

On July 13, 1944, SS Hauptsturmführer (Captain) Michael Wittmann rolled forwards in his Tiger, engaging a column of the British 7th Armored Division in the French town of Villers-Bocage. Within minutes, his Tiger had wreaked havoc and, by the time other tanks of his SS Heavy Panzer Battalion 101 had finished their work, at least 13 British tanks, two anti-tank guns, and up to 15 troop carriers and support vehicles had been destroyed. Accounts of the action at Villers-Bocage vary, but the conclusion is obvious. As a fighting vehicle, the Tiger was supreme on the battlefields of World War II.

Interior view

The interior of the Tiger tank included several notable revisions from earlier German tank designs, including a reorientation of the famed 3.5-in (88-mm) multi-purpose cannon to fit within the turret.

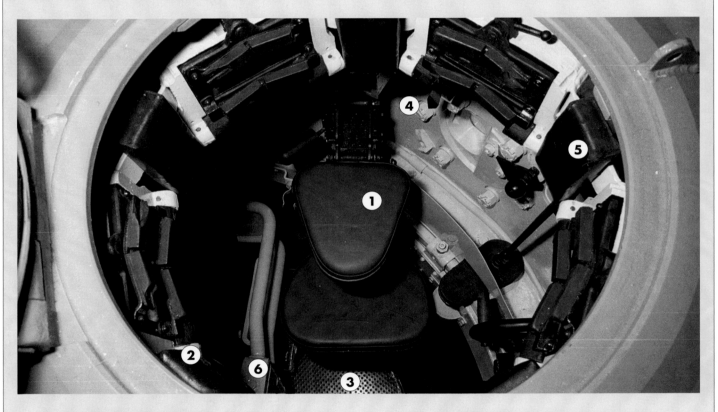

(1) **Commander's Seat:** The commander's seat, which folded to allow extra space during combat operations, was located on the left side of the 3.5-in (88-mm) cannon breech.

(2) **Ammunition Storage:** 92 rounds of armor-piercing and high-explosive 3.5-in (88-mm) shells were stored beneath the turret floor and passed to the loader as needed.

(3) **Turret Basket:** The 360-degree circular floor of the Tiger's 11-ton (9.9-tonne) turret had only cramped space for three crewmen.

(4) **Armor Plating:** Heavy armor protection throughout the vehicle made the Tiger virtually impervious to most ordnance.

(5) **Optical and Communications Equipment:** The commander of the Tiger tank used advanced optics and communications equipment to acquire targets.

(6) **Weapon Configuration:** The bulk of the 3.5-in (88-mm) cannon took up a great deal of space within the turret, protruding to the rear of the compartment.

Covered with anti-mine Zimmerit paste, a Tiger tank pauses on a dirt road on the Western Front. Two crewmen have emerged from their hatches. The main drawback of this powerful tank was that there were never enough of them for the German army to deploy.

Among Allied troops, the Tiger, first deployed in North Africa in late 1942, gained a fearsome reputation. To many British and American soldiers, every German tank they observed on the battlefield was thought to be a Tiger. Allied tank crewmen respected the Tiger as well. "All you saw in your imagination was the muzzle of an 88 behind each leaf," recalled British tank commander Andrew Wilson.

VIRTUALLY UNBEATABLE

The mere presence of the Henschel-designed Tiger tank could alter the course of a battle. It is estimated that the Tiger achieved a kill ratio approaching six to one against Allied tanks. Its 3.5-in (88-mm) cannon, with a muzzle velocity of up to 3051 ft (930 m) per second, could penetrate the frontal armor of an U.S. Sherman or British Churchill IV tank at a distance of more than a mile and the Soviet T-34 at slightly closer range. Its Zeiss optics, improved steering and transmission, and heavier armor protection were a huge leap forward in tank design. Favoring firepower and armor over maneuverability, the Tiger was virtually unbeatable in single combat on suitable terrain in ideal weather conditions, but rarely were such circumstances assured.

For all its combat capabilities, particularly in the hands of a seasoned commander, the Tiger suffered from numerous mechanical problems, particularly with its overlapping wheels and suspension system, and an initially inadequate powerplant. Its sheer weight made transport, deployment, and routine maintenance challenging. Rushed into production, the Tiger was put through its paces during trials in a cursory manner at best. Further, the complexity of the vehicle resulted in prohibitive cost per unit, roughly equal to that of four PzKpfw III assault guns. Limited production capability meant that slightly fewer than 1350 were built before production ceased in 1944 in favor of the Tiger II. In contrast, more than 40,000 U.S. Sherman tanks and nearly 60,000 Soviet T-34s were produced in that time period.

In addition to Wittmann – a holder of the Knights Cross with Oak Leaves and Swords who was killed in action two months after his stand at Villers-Bocage – numerous Tiger tank commanders racked up impressive scores of enemy vehicles destroyed. At least a dozen claimed to have more than 100 kills. Considering that it was rarely available in large numbers, the combat record of the Tiger tank is all the more impressive and deservedly legendary.

IS-3 Josef Stalin

The Josef Stalin series of heavy tanks was intended to maintain a perceived Soviet superiority in tank design on the Eastern Front during World War II. The IS-3, developed late in the war, was the world's most powerful tank during the early years of the Cold War.

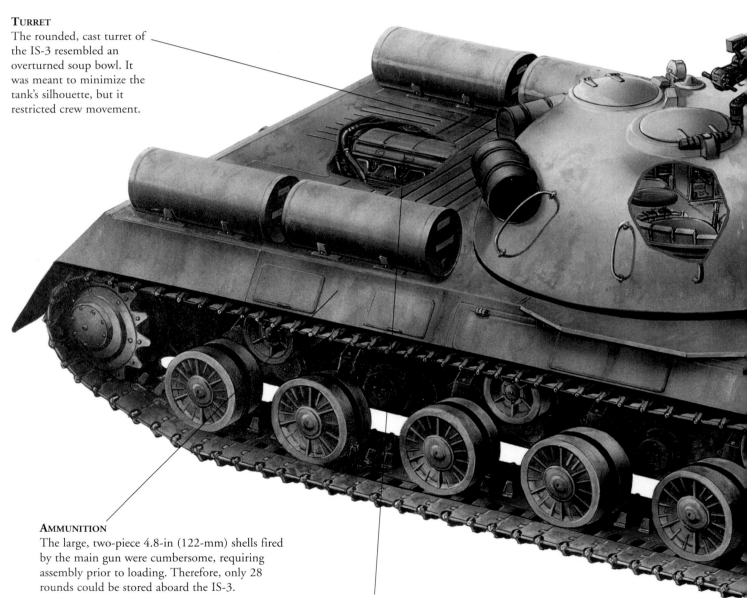

TURRET
The rounded, cast turret of the IS-3 resembled an overturned soup bowl. It was meant to minimize the tank's silhouette, but it restricted crew movement.

AMMUNITION
The large, two-piece 4.8-in (122-mm) shells fired by the main gun were cumbersome, requiring assembly prior to loading. Therefore, only 28 rounds could be stored aboard the IS-3.

ENGINE
The IS-3 was powered by a 12-cylinder, V-2 diesel engine generating 600 hp (447 kW).

SECONDARY ARMAMENT
The IS-3 was further armed with 0.5-in (12.7-mm) or 0.3-in (7.62-mm) machine guns.

BREECH
Unable to pivot fully on its vertical axis, the breech of the main gun limited the ability to depress the weapon completely.

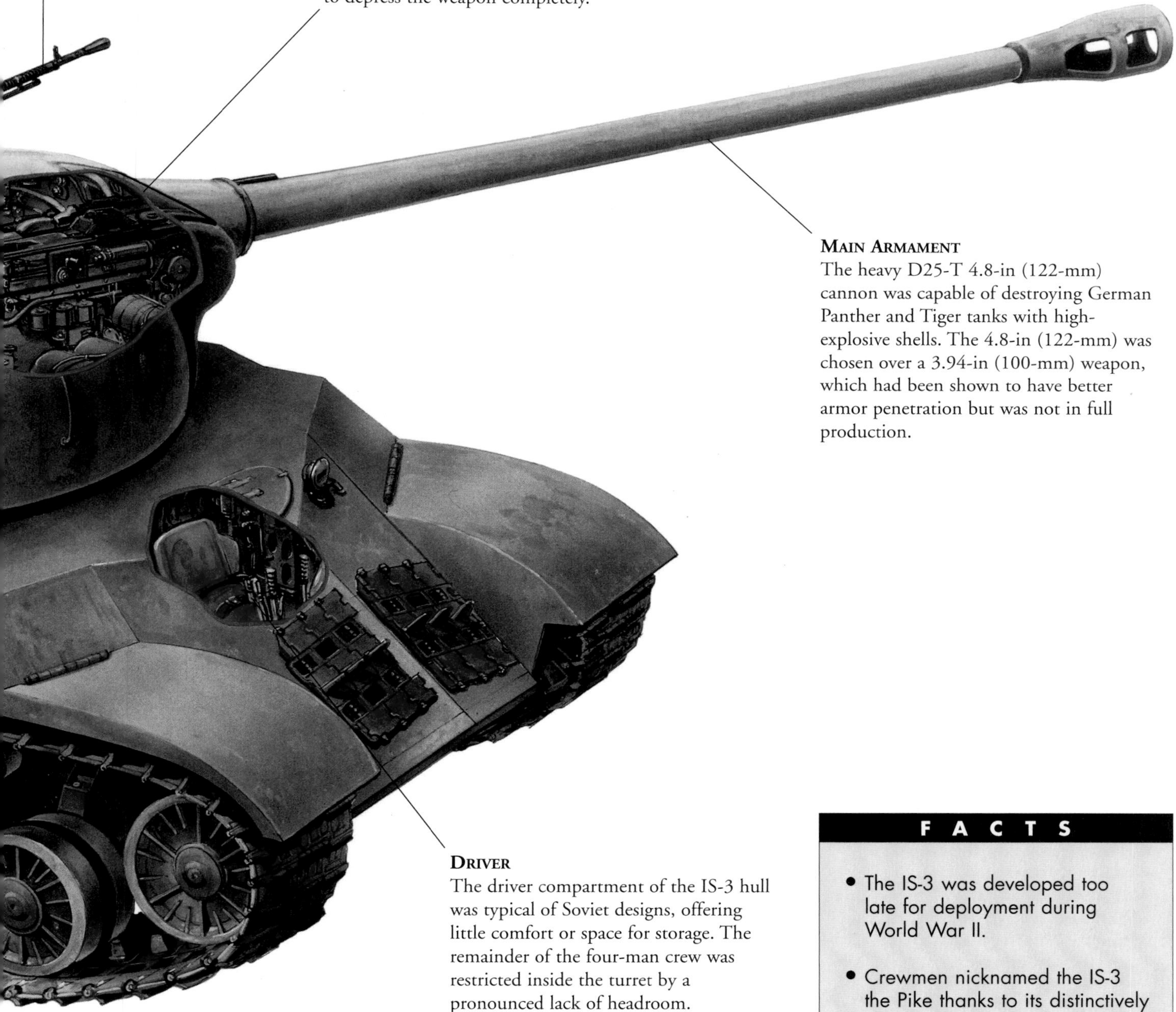

MAIN ARMAMENT
The heavy D25-T 4.8-in (122-mm) cannon was capable of destroying German Panther and Tiger tanks with high-explosive shells. The 4.8-in (122-mm) was chosen over a 3.94-in (100-mm) weapon, which had been shown to have better armor penetration but was not in full production.

DRIVER
The driver compartment of the IS-3 hull was typical of Soviet designs, offering little comfort or space for storage. The remainder of the four-man crew was restricted inside the turret by a pronounced lack of headroom.

FACTS

- The IS-3 was developed too late for deployment during World War II.

- Crewmen nicknamed the IS-3 the Pike thanks to its distinctively pointed hull design.

- The IS-3 formed the basis for Soviet tank designs of the Cold War era.

A special commission was formed in 1943 to analyze the reasons for the horrendous losses suffered by Soviet military tank units in the Battle of Kursk. A total of 6064 machines had been lost during the 38 days of battle. In response, a new heavy tank, the IS-3, was designed.

IS-3 JOSEF STALIN – SPECIFICATION

Country of origin: USSR
Crew: 4
Designer: Zh. Kotin, N. Dukhov
Designed: 1944
In service: 1943–1970s
Manufacturer: Kirov Factory, UZTM
Number built: 2311
Produced: 1943–47
Gross Weight: 50.4 tons (45.8 tonnes)

Dimensions:
Hull Length: 22.2 ft (6.77 m)
Length (gun forward): 32.25 ft (9.83 m)
Width: 10.1 ft (3.07 m)
Overall Height: 8 ft (2.44 m)

Performance:
Maximum Speed: 23 mph (37 km/h)
Range, Road: 100 miles (160 km)
Range, Cross-country: 75 miles (120 km)
Ground Pressure: 0.83 kg/cm²
Fording Capacity: 4.3 ft (1.3 m)
Maximum Gradient: 30 degrees
Maximum Trench Width: 8.2 ft (2.5 m)
Maximum Vertical Obstacle: 3.3 ft (1 m)
Suspension Type: Torsion bars

Engine:
Powerplant: V-2-IS V-12 water-cooled diesel engine
Capacity: 8.6 gallons (38.9 l)
Output: 600 bhp (447 kW)
Power/Weight Ratio: 11.35 bhp/ton
Fuel Capacity: 114 gallons (520 l); +66 gallons (300 l)

Armament and Armor:
Main Armament: 1 x 4.8-in (122-mm) L/43 D-25 (M1943)
Secondary Armament: 2 x 0.3-in (7.62-mm) DT or DTM MG
Ancillary Armament: 0.5-in (12.7-mm) DShK MG on AA mount
Armor Type: Homogeneous rolled/welded and cast nickel-steel
Hull Front: 3.6–4.7 in (90–120 mm)
Hull Sides: 3.8 in (95 mm)
Hull Rear: 2.4 in (60 mm)
Hull Top: 0.8–1.2 in (20–30 mm)
Hull Bottom: 0.8–1.2 in (20–30 mm)
Turret Front: 9 in (230 mm)
Turret Sides: 3.9–6.3 in (100–160 mm)
Turret Rear: 3.6 in (90 mm)
Turret Top: 1.2 in (30 mm)

Other Variants:
IS-85 (IS-1): 1943 model armed with an 3.35-in (85-mm) gun.
IS-100: A prototype version armed with a 3.94-in (100-mm) gun.
IS-122 (IS-2 model 1943): Production model with A-19 4.8-in (122-mm) gun.
IS-2 model 1944 (sometimes "IS-2m"): 1944 improvement with D25-T 4.8-in (122-mm) gun.
IS-2M: 1950s modernization of IS-2 tanks.
IS-3M: (1952) Modernized version of IS-3.
IS-4: 1944 design, in competition against the IS-3. Longer hull and thicker armor than IS-2.
IS-7 model 1948: 1946 prototype, only three built. Crew of five.
IS-10: 1952 improvement with a longer hull, seven pairs of road wheels instead of six, a larger turret mounting a new gun with fume extractor, an improved diesel engine, and increased armor. Renamed T-10.

IS-3 JOSEF STALIN

Incorporating a heavy 4.8-in (122-mm) cannon, the IS-3 was the latest Soviet tank design of World War II. However, it was not deployed during the war. A welded hull of rolled steel plating was sloped to the maximum degree, and the frontal area of the tank was substantially reduced from its predecessor, the IS-2. The thickness of the frontal hull armor was increased to 4.7 in (120 mm), while the turret thickness was raised to 9 in (230 mm). The turret was dramatically rounded and flattened, reducing the silhouette at the expense of crew space and the ability of the main weapon to fully depress.

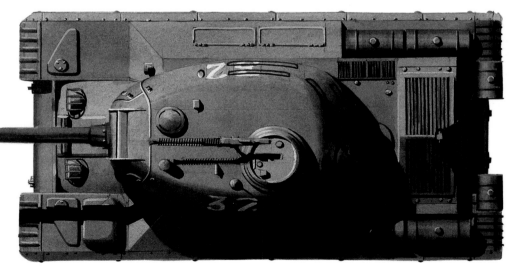

The IS-3 heavy tank was the final Soviet design of the World War II era. It was not deployed during the war, but served as a symbol of excellence in Soviet Cold War tank design.

In late 1944, the IS-2 design was upgraded to the IS-3. This tank had improved armor layout and a hemispherical cast turret, resembling an overturned soup bowl, which was to be the hallmark of postwar Soviet tanks.

Some reports indicate that the Soviet IS-3 heavy tank may have been deployed in quite limited numbers during World War II, possibly against the Japanese in Manchuria in 1945. However, no official documentation of such an event is known to exist. Nevertheless, the IS-3, named in honor of Soviet premier Josef Stalin, represented the pinnacle of Soviet armored design during the war and provided a foretaste of a design philosophy that would go on to dominate Eastern bloc production throughout the Cold War.

The Soviet T-34 medium and KV-1 heavy tanks had, by 1943, enabled the Red Army to seize the initiative on the Eastern Front. While the T-34 became a combat legend, the KV-1 and its later variant, the KV-85, were the subjects of

considerable modification. A retooling of the transmission and suspension, coupled with a redesigned turret and hull configuration, evolved the tank into more than a new variant of the KV-1. The new armored fighting vehicle was designated the IS-1, mounting a 3.35-in (85-mm) main cannon identical to that of the KV-85. As the new tank developed, it was apparent that it could accommodate a heavier gun, and trials were conducted with a 3.94-in (100-mm) and a 4.8-in (122-mm) gun. The former offered better armor penetration capability, but the latter was chosen because of the explosive power of its round and ready availability. In time, the 4.8-in (122-mm) proved to be a deadly efficient anti-personnel round.

MORE ARMOR, REDUCED WEIGHT

By 1944, the IS-2 had entered service, mounting the 4.8-in (122-mm) cannon and introducing reconfigured armor plating, which provided virtually the same protection for tank and crew but reduced the overall weight. However, the two components of the heavy 4.8-in (122-mm) shell had to be assembled prior to loading, significantly slowing the rate of fire. The original 4.8-in (122-mm) gun, the A-19, was replaced subsequently by the D25-T, with a double baffle muzzle brake, which had a better rate of fire and improved fire control and coordination. Additional improvements to later IS-2 models included a turret-mounted anti-aircraft machine gun and a hull configuration without a step-up to the front.

FUTURE SHAPE

Production of the IS-3 began in May 1945 under the direction of M.F. Balzha at Soviet Experimental Plant No. 100 and concluded a year later. By the end of World War II, fewer than 30 IS-3s had been built, but by mid-1946, IS-3s in service totalled more than 2300. The tank control system enabled the commander to rotate the turret, and its flattened design and bow-shaped forward hull looked sleek, yet it was less able to take advantage of hull-down tactics as a result.

The IS-3 did not participate in operations during World War II, but a regiment was paraded through Moscow on September 7, 1945. The IS-3 was considered the world's most powerful tank for years to come, and its initial appearance gave Western military leaders reason to pause.

Close-up

The design of the IS-3 Josef Stalin heavy tank did little to improve internal ergonomics or the comfort of its crew. The distinctive turret offered little headroom for three crewmen.

(1) **Handle Assists:** Handles on the turret allowed infantrymen and maintenance personnel to enter and exit the tank easily.

(2) **Rear Hatches:** A pair of circular hatches allowed access to and from the IS-3 hull at the rear of the tank and facilitated the loading of ammunition and supplies.

(3) **Top Hatches:** Two rectangular hatches on top of the rear hull, sited just behind the turret, allowed crewmen rapid entry and exit.

(4) **Commander's Cupola:** This was often equipped with either a 0.5-in (12.7-mm) or 0.3-in (7.62-mm) ring-mounted machine gun.

(5) **Fuel Barrels:** In keeping with tanks of the Soviet Red Army deployed previously, the IS-3 Josef Stalin carried fuel barrels secured externally to its elongated hull.

(6) **Sloped Armor:** The hull and turret armor of this heavy tank featured a pronounced slope, increasing protective thickness.

Centurion A41

Britain drew upon its experience of having had to fight against superior armor during World War II when it created the Centurion A41 main battle tank. More than a dozen variants, or Marks, were produced during a post-war length of service that spanned more than 50 years.

COMMANDER POSITION
Situated on the right side of the turret under a rotating cupola, the Centurion commander led a crew of four. His periscopic rangefinding sights were mechanically linked to those of the gunner.

ENGINE
The original powerplant of the Centurion A41 was the 650-hp (485-kW), 12-cylinder Rolls Royce Mark IVB engine, while the subsequent Israeli-improved Centurion was powered by the 900-hp (485-kW) Teledyne Continental AVDS-1790-2R diesel engine.

ARMOR PROTECTION
The maximum thickness of the welded steel hull was 4.72 in (120 mm), intended originally to withstand the heavy 3.5-in (88-mm) shells of German tanks during World War II.

FACTS

- A total of 4423 Centurion tanks were built from 1945–62.
- Although the Centurion was built to 1943 specifications, it only entered service after World War II had ended.
- Modified Centurions remained in service as support vehicles as late as 2006.

SECONDARY ARMAMENT
A 0.3-in (7.62-mm) caliber Browning machine gun was mounted coaxially in the turret. A second 0.3-in (7.62-mm) caliber machine gun was mounted in the hull, and a 0.5-in (12.7-mm) caliber Browning M2 anti-aircraft machine gun was situated on top of the turret. Other options included an early 0.78-in (20-mm) cannon and smoke grenade launchers.

DRIVER COMPARTMENT
The driver compartment, forwards and to the right, was equipped with two periscopes for forwards observation. Ammunition was stored to the driver's left.

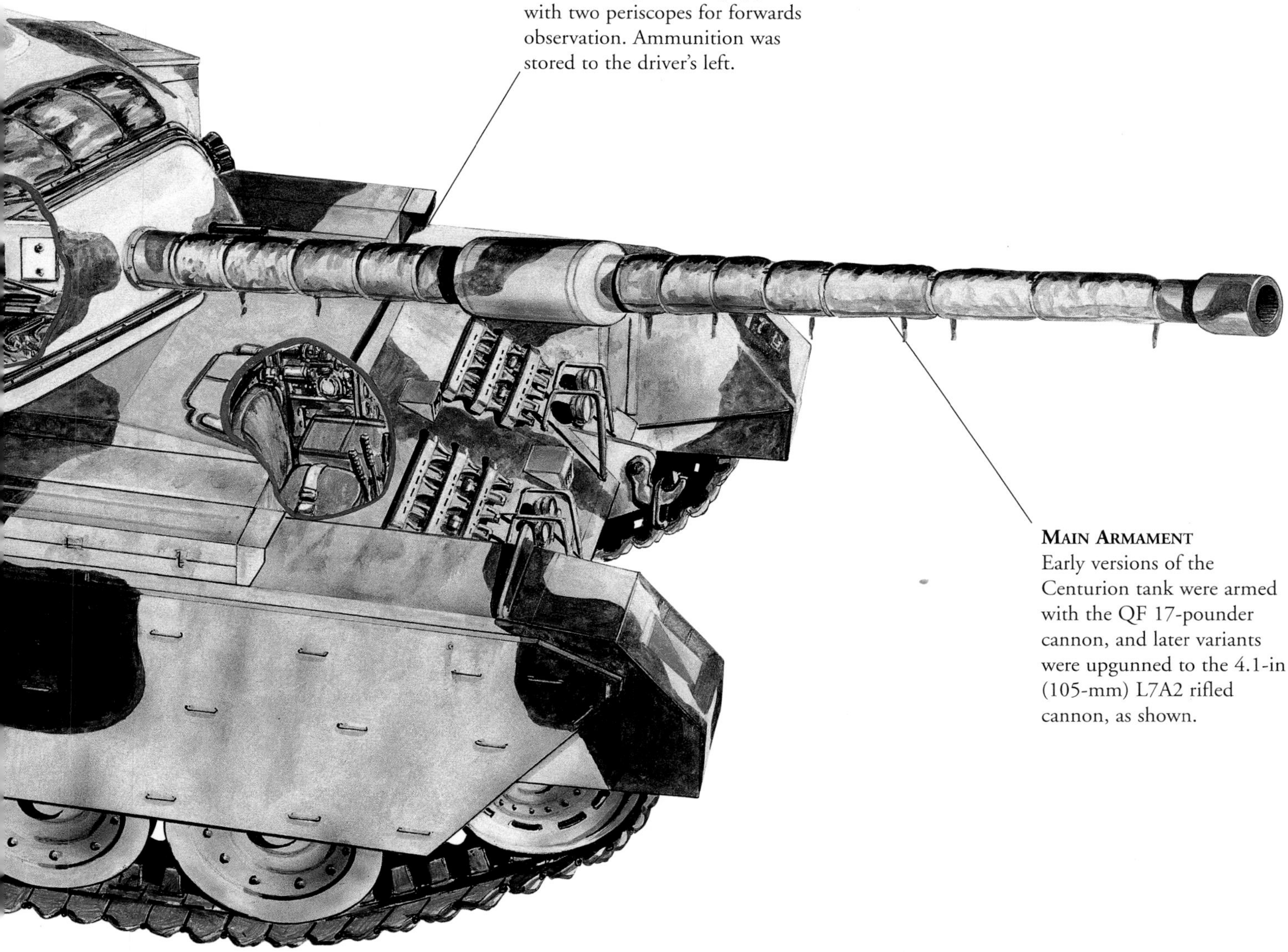

MAIN ARMAMENT
Early versions of the Centurion tank were armed with the QF 17-pounder cannon, and later variants were upgunned to the 4.1-in (105-mm) L7A2 rifled cannon, as shown.

The Centurion was replaced by the Chieftain in the British army itself, but at least 2400 are still in service. The Centurion's longevity is a tribute to the soundness of the basic design, including its ability to incorporate a host of modifications.

CENTURION A41 – SPECIFICATION

Country of Origin: United Kingdom
Crew: 4
Designer: Department of Tank Design
Designed: 1943–45
Manufacturers: Leyland, Royal Ordnance Factories, Vickers
In Production: 1945–62
In Service: 1946–90s (derivatives still in service)
Number Produced: 4423
Weight: 57 tons (52 tonnes)

Dimensions:
Hull Length: 25 ft (7.6 m)
Length (gun forward): 32 ft 4 in (9.85 m)
Width: 11 ft 1 in (3.38 m)
Height: 9 ft 10.5 in (3.01 m)

Performance:
Speed: 21 mph (34 km/h)
Operational range: 280 miles (450 km)
Gradient: 60 degrees
Maximum Vertical Obstacle: 3 ft (0.91 m)
Maximum Trench Width: 11 ft (3.35 m)

Engine:
Powerplant: 1 x Rolls-Royce Meteor 650 hp (485 kW)
Power/Weight Ratio: 13 hp/ton
Suspension: Horstmann suspension

Armor and Armament:
Armor: 6 in (150 mm)
Main Armament: 4.1-in (105-mm) L7A2 rifled gun
    17-pounder, 20-pounder
Secondary Armament: 0.3-in (7.62-mm) Browning machine gun

Major UK variants:
Mark 1: 17-pounder armed version.
Mark 2: Fully cast turret.
Mark 3: Fitted with 20-pounder, 2 storage positions for track links.
Mark 4: Projected close-support version with 3.74-in (95-mm) CS howitzer.
Mark 5: Browning machine guns fitted to coaxial and commander's cupola mounts, storage bin on glacis.
Mark 6: Upgunned and uparmored Mark 5.
Mark 7 aka FV 4007: Revised engine decks.
Mark 8: Resilient mantlet and new commander's cupola.
Mark 9 (aka FV 4015): Upgunned and uparmored Mark 7.
Mark 10 (aka FV 4017): Upgunned and uparmored Mark 8.
Mark 11: Mark 6 fitted with IR equipment and ranging gun.
Mark 12: Mark 9 fitted with IR equipment and ranging gun.
AVRE 105: Combat Engineer Version with 4.1-in (105-mm) gun.
AVRE 165: Combat Engineer Version with 6.5-in (165-mm) gun.
BARV: Beach Armored Recovery Vehicle.
Bridgelayer aka FV 4002: Class 80 bridgelayer.

CENTURION SHO'T

The Centurion design is considered one of the best of the post–World War II era, and the Israeli Sho't variant (shown) remained in service into the 1990s. Armed with the 4.13-in (105-mm) L7 cannon, the Sho't gained fame during the Yom Kippur War of 1973, battling Syrian T-54/55 and T-62 tanks. The Centurion incorporated a Horstmann suspension of external horizontal springs, a welded hull of sloped armor, and turret armor of 6 in (152 mm). The driver was seated in the bow with the commander in the turret above the fighting compartment at center, and the engine compartment to the rear. The gunner was situated below and in front of the commander, while the loader served the main weapon from his left.

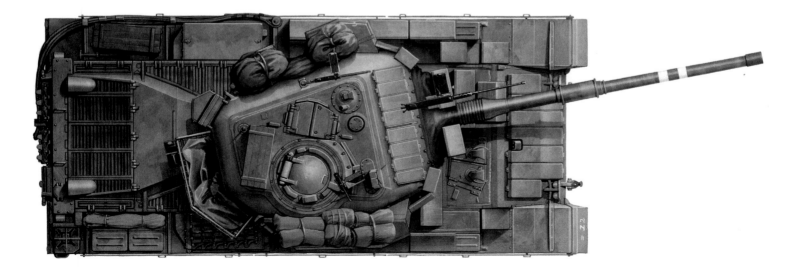

In one of the few instances on record, the War Ministry decided it would be a better idea to build new trailers than hamper a superb design. Even before prototypes of the original 40-ton (36-tonne) design were completed, a heavier version was well under way.

The eventual weight of the British Centurion A41 main battle tank was to reach 52 tons (45 tonnes) but the need for heavier trailers to transport the behemoth was considered a reasonable tradeoff by the Department of Tank Design. The Centurion measured up so well to its other specifications that it was considered by many to be the "universal tank."

Initially, the Centurion A41 was the response to the War Ministry's 1943 requirement for a British tank that could take on heavy German armor on the battlefields of World War II. In the event, it reached the continent of Europe in

Interior view

The turret's mechanical apparatus and power generation systems were located below the turret basket and crew areas, making them easily accessible for routine maintenance or repairs.

1. **Electric Transversing Motor:** The electric transversing motor and transmission supplied power to the broad shaft in the background.

2. **Air Collection:** The collection and filtering of air within the turret reduced the possible build-up of noxious fumes.

3. **Hydraulic Lines:** Hydraulics and electrical lines powered the turret and were used to adjust the elevation of the main weapon, and operate other systems.

4. **Armor Protection:** The hull of the Centurion tank was made of welded steel up to 4 in (120 mm) thick to defend against the high velocity German 3.46-in (88-mm) shell.

5. **Transversing Gears:** The teeth of the transversing gears are visible in a circular pattern at the base of the turret.

6. **Elevation Apparatus:** The elevation of the main weapon was controlled by the apparatus shown in the foreground.

Crewmen of a Centurion tank change one of the armored vehicle's drive sprockets in the field. The Centurion was developed during World War II but arrived too late to see action. However, it became a tank of great standing in the Cold War era.

May 1945, only days after the conflict had ended. All the effort in its creation did not go to waste, though, because the Centurion went on to become one of the most enduring tank designs of the Cold War era.

During nearly two decades of production by the Royal Ordnance Factory, Leyland, Vickers, and other companies, no fewer than 12 variants of the original Centurion were produced. A total of 4423 were manufactured, and the Israeli Defense Force became the largest single user with more than 1100 in service.

Early Centurions were armed with the QF 17-pounder anti-tank gun, while a relative few mounted the 20-pounder, and later the 4-in (105-mm) L7A2 rifled gun became the standard. Through the years, armored protection increased from 3 in (76 mm) in the Mark 1 to 4.7 in (120 mm) in the welded steel plate hull and more than 5.9 in (150 mm) in the turret. Prominent among the variants were the Centurion Mark 2, which included better armor protection, and the Mark 3, fitted with an automated gun stabilizer. The Mark 5 was the first to mount the 4-in (105-mm) main armament.

Although the all-round performance of the Centurion exceeded expectations, its limited range, relatively low road speed of 21 mph (34 km/h), and merely average cross-country capabilities were its most prominent drawbacks. The Israelis actually improved the Centurion's performance by fitting the tank with a larger Teledyne Continental diesel engine, which gave it greater fuel and ammunition capacity. They also fitted the tank with superior fire-control equipment.

COLD WAR VETERAN

The combat record of the Centurion A41 can justifiably be considered superb. During the Korean War, the 8th King's Royal Irish Hussars covered the retreat of the outnumbered 29th Infantry Brigade at the Battle of the Imjin River and earned high praise from General John O'Daniel, commander of the U.S. I Corps, who commented that the "8th Hussars have evolved a new type of tank warfare. They taught us that anywhere a tank can go is tank country – even the tops of mountains."

During the Vietnam War, the Royal Australian Armored Corps deployed 58 Centurion tanks, while the Centurions of the Indian army outclassed American tanks supplied to Pakistani forces during the wars of 1965 and 1971. The Israelis deployed Centurions during the Six-Day War of 1967, the Yom Kippur War of 1973, and later incursions into Lebanon. In Korea and Southeast Asia, however, the Centurion was limited in its deployment because of its weight, which was too great for most bridges.

The longevity of the Centurion A41, along with its proven combat effectiveness, make the design one of the best of the latter half of the twentieth century.

T-54/55

Produced in greater numbers than any other tank in history, the Soviet T-54/55 series was developed as a successor to the T-44, which had been a disappointing attempt to improve the famed T-34 of World War II. The service life of the T-54/55 exceeds half a century.

FIRE CONTROL
Early models of the T-54/55 were equipped with manual target-acquisition systems. These were replaced with automated systems on later models, but even these were not as good as contemporary NATO aiming devices.

MAIN ARMAMENT
The original armament of the T-54/55 series was the D-10T 3.94-in (100-mm) rifled cannon. This gun eventually proved inferior to more modern weapons and was replaced by the D-10T2S with a bore evacuator located near the muzzle.

ARMOR PROTECTION
Even though it was relatively lightly armored, the T-54/55 provided turret crew with the protection of 8-in (203-mm) armor, while the front glacis was 3.94 in (100 mm) thick and the sides 2.75 in (70 mm) thick.

- More than 80,000 were manufactured before production ended in 1981.

- The T-54/55 series was produced in the Soviet Union, Czechoslovakia, and Poland, while an unlicensed version was made in China.

- The tank was considerably smaller than contemporary main battle tanks of Western design.

TURRET
The low silhouette of the T-54/55 was made possible by the turret design, resembling an overturned frying pan. However, the confined space inside, along with the absence of a turret basket in earlier models, made operating the tank exhausting for three of the four crewmen.

SUSPENSION
The modified Christie suspension did not provide return rollers, while tracks were replaced twice as often as those of contemporary Western tanks. The tracks were also prone to being thrown at higher speeds.

ENGINE
The 520-hp (388-kW) V-2-54 diesel engine of the early T-54 was prone to failure and catching fire because of metal filings clogging oil lines. Built primarily of magnesium alloy, it was replaced with a larger V-12 engine in the T-55.

Its armament, design, and construction are often considered inferior to the tanks of other nations, yet the T-54/55 was always available in large numbers. Its production was nearly three times that of U.S. tanks manufactured from 1945–80.

T-54

T-54/55 – SPECIFICATION

Country of Origin: Soviet Union
Crew: 4
Designer: Not Specified
Designed: Not Specified
In Production: 1948–78
Manufacturers: Various
In Service: 1948–present
Number Built: 95,000
Gross Weight: 39.6 tons (36 tonnes)

Dimensions:
Hull Length: 21.15 ft (6.45 m)
Length (gun forward): 29.5 ft (9 m)
Width: 10.7 ft (3.27 m)
Overall Height: 7.85 ft (2.4 m)

Performance:
Range, Road: 300 miles (500 km)
Range, Cross-country: 180 miles (300 km)
Maximum Speed: 30 mph (50 km/h)
Ground Pressure: 0.81 kg/cm²
Fording Capacity: 4.6 ft (1.4 m) (Submersible to 18 ft [5.5 m] with preparation)
Maximum Gradient: 30 degrees
Maximum Trench Width: 8.9 ft (2.7 m)
Maximum Vertical Obstacle: 2.6 ft (0.8 m)
Suspension Type: Torsion bar

Engine:
Powerplant: 1 x Type V-54 V-12 water-cooled diesel engine
Capacity: n/a
Output: 520 hp (388 kW) @ 2000 rpm

Power/Weight Ratio: 16.1 bhp/ton
Fuel Capacity: 211.5 gallons (960 l)

Armament and Armor:
Main Armament: 1 x 3.94-in (100-mm) D-10T2S L/54 gun
Secondary Armament: 0.3-in (7.62-mm) PKT MG in coaxial mount
Ancillary Armament: 0.5-in (12.7-mm) DShKM MG in AA mount
Armor Type: Homogeneous rolled/welded with cast turret
Hull Front: 4 in (100 mm)
Hull Sides: 2.8 in (70 mm)
Hull Rear: 2.4 in (60 mm)
Hull Top: 1.2 in (30 mm)
Hull Bottom: 0.8 in (20 mm)
Turret Front: 4–6.8 in (100–170 mm)
Turret Sides: 4 in (100 mm)
Turret Rear: 4 in (100 mm)
Turret Top: 2.8 in (70 mm)

Variants:
T-54A: Fitted with 3.94-in (100-mm) main gun with fume extractor, deep water equipment, and gun stabilizer on vertical plane.
T-54AK: Command tank.
T-54M: T-54 models upgraded to T-55 standard.
T-54B: With infrared night vision equipment.
T-54C: Some without AA gun; later retrofitted.
T-55M: Without loader's cupola.
T-54K: Command vehicle.
T-54 ARV: Armored Recovery Vehicle utilizing T-54 chassis.
T-54 AVLB: Bridge layer variant utilizing T-54 chassis.
T-54 IMR: Combat engineer vehicle utilizing T-54 chassis.
Type 59: Chinese production model designation.
TI-67: Israeli conversion model.
T-54AD: Polish designation of T-54AK command tank.

VARIANT: T-55

T-54/55

When the T-44 proved an unworthy late wartime successor to the legendary T-34/85 medium tank, its hull was topped with a sleek, dome-shaped turret and a 4-in (100-mm) cannon in the prototype of the T-54 main battle tank. By the late 1950s, so many modifications had been made that a new designation, T-55, was given to a version with an improved main weapon and more powerful engine. Still, the shortcomings of the T-54/55 design persisted, most notably the confined turret space with three crewmen on the same side and the loader required to perform an exhausting series of movements to service the main gun.

VARIANT: T-55

The T-54 and T-55 tanks are outwardly very similar and difficult to distinguish visually. Many T-54s were also updated to T-55 standards, and the distinction is often downplayed with the collective name T-54/55. Numerous variants of both tanks are in service today.

The T-54/55 main battle tank remains the backbone of the armored forces of many former Warsaw Pact and Third World countries. Since 1949, more than 80,000 have been produced, and the basic design has served in combat in the deserts of the Middle East and the jungles of Africa and Southeast Asia.

At 39.6 tons (36 tonnes), the T-54/55 was lighter than other main battle tanks of the Cold War era, and its armor protection was inferior to that of potential opponents. The effectiveness of the original main gun, the 3.94-in (100-mm)

Close-up

The Soviet tank designers' neglect of crew comfort and operational space inside the tank continued with the T-54/55, the first post–World War II tank exported by the Soviet Union.

(1) **Turret Hatch:** One of two hatches on top of the turret, the commander's hatch was affixed to a slightly raised cupola.

(2) **Periscopes:** These ringed the turret cupola, allowing the commander a broad view of the field before him.

(3) **Telescopic Sight:** Telescopic sights were used by both the gunner and commander to acquire targets and assess the terrain over which their T-54/55 tank was maneuvering.

(4) **Turret Armor:** Though the turret armor was thick at 8 in (203 mm) in the front, it measured only 1.5 in (39 mm) on top.

(5) **Turret Seal:** The tight turret seal of later variants of the T-54/55 tank was an essential component of defense against nuclear, chemical, and biological agents.

(6) **Bolted Construction:** Some variants of this tank have bolted, rather than cast, cupolas for both the commander and the gunner.

The pintle-mounted 0.5-in (12.7-mm) anti-aircraft machine gun of the T-54/55 fires rapidly during exercises. More than 80,000 variants of the ubiquitous Soviet main battle tank were built during a period of more than three decades.

D10T, which was adapted from a dual-purpose naval weapon, was limited due to the lack of a computerized fire-control system. Its top-loading breech was a handicap, seriously reducing its rate of fire. Later, the D-10T2S, with a bore evacuator and improved gun-laying system, were installed. Secondary armament first consisted of a coaxial 0.3-in (7.62-mm) machine gun, a remote-controlled, hull-mounted 0.3-in (7.62-mm) machine gun, as well as a 0.5-in (12.7-mm) pintle-mounted machine gun near the loader's hatch.

The design of the T-54 is similar to other Soviet-era tanks, with an engine compartment to the rear, driver compartment forwards, and low, cramped turret that hampers the traverse of the main cannon. One of the most serious limitations of the T-54 was the design of the turret interior. Three crewmen, the commander, gunner, and loader, were all on the left side and could all be taken out by a single hit. The driver was situated in the centerline of the hull. Fuel and ammunition were in close proximity to each other, also posing an extraordinary danger to vehicle survivability.

STEADY IMPROVEMENT

Further, the seats on the early T-54 were welded to the hull, and the turret floor did not rotate with the turret itself. Therefore, the loader was required to pull rounds from storage while avoiding the breech as the turret rotated. He then had to place a shell into the breech with his left hand. By the mid-1950s, improvements to the T-54 included a stabilized main gun and a nuclear, biological, and chemical (NBC) defense system. This variant was designated T-54A. In the subsequent T-54B, the 3.94-in (100-mm) D-10T2S gun was stabilized in two planes, and by 1960, the T-54C was notable for the removal of one of the machine guns and a loader's hatch, which was flush with the turret. Certain tanks have been equipped with a snorkel and can traverse up to 18 ft (5.5 m) of water.

In 1958, the T-55 emerged as the latest variant in the T-54 series. The primary distinguishing features of the T-55 included the absence of a loader's cupola and a turret dome ventilator, as well as the removal, in most cases, of the turret-mounted 0.5-in (12.7-mm) machine gun. Its 580-hp (432-kW) V-12 water-cooled V-2-55 diesel engine was an improvement over that of the T-54, but it was still prone to mechanical failure because of inferior manufacture. The T-55 did incorporate a turret basket, greatly improving the main gun's efficiency. Further improvements with the T-55 included a modestly increased ammunition capacity, better fire control with the introduction of a laser rangefinder, and enhanced armor protection.

While the T-54/55 is largely outmoded, its great numbers and adaptability to upgrades have increased its longevity.

M48 Patton

Cold War battles against Soviet tanks in Europe were seen as a real possibility when this tank was conceptualized. The third in the Patton series of U.S. medium tanks, the M48 was designed to be an improvement over its immediate predecessor, the M47.

TURRET
Three crew – the commander, gunner, and loader – sat in the turret. The commander was situated high and to the right with the loader to his left, while the gunner sat below the commander. The turret itself was elliptical in shape, and had a maximum armor protection of 4.3 in (110 mm).

FIRE CONTROL
The fire-control system of the M48A3 was highly specialized for its time in the 1960s. A system of mirrors found range and fed data into a ballistic computer.

HULL CONSTRUCTION
The improved hull of the M48 included a bowl-shaped bottom and sloping top sides. Previous designs had a welded, box-like construction.

FACTS

- The M48 was deployed to Somalia by Pakistani peacekeepers in the 1990s.
- From 1952–59, more than 12,000 M48 tanks were built.
- The service career of the M48 spans over half a century. The tank was deployed in conflicts in Vietnam and the Middle East.

SEARCHLIGHT
Sighted with the main gun and gunsights, a xenon searchlight with one million candle power functioned in both infrared and standard modes to illuminate targets.

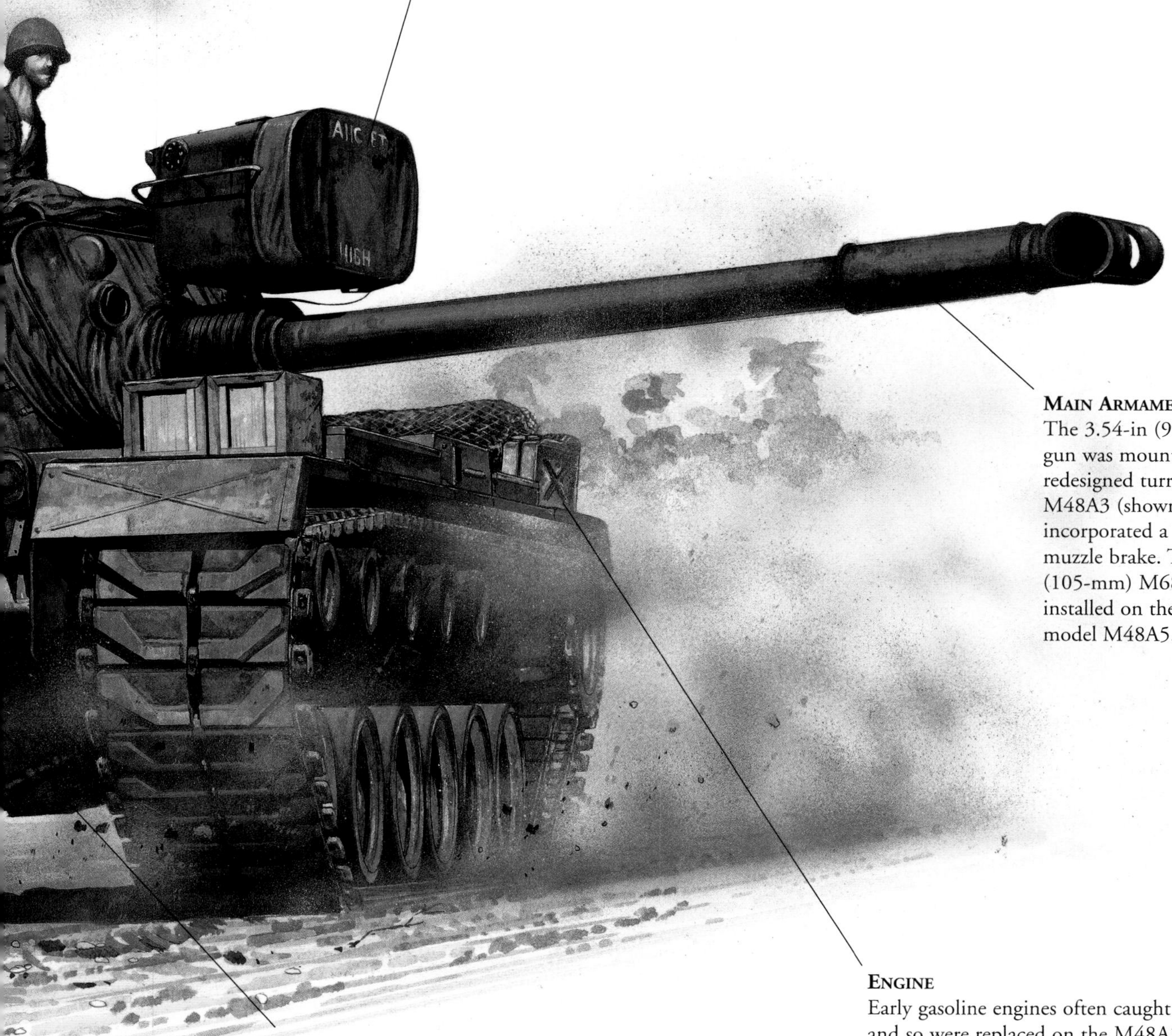

MAIN ARMAMENT
The 3.54-in (90-mm) M41 gun was mounted in the redesigned turret of the M48A3 (shown) and incorporated a T-shaped muzzle brake. The 4-in (105-mm) M68 cannon was installed on the later model M48A5.

ENGINE
Early gasoline engines often caught fire and so were replaced on the M48A3 with the 750-hp (560-kW) Continental AVDS-1790-2A diesel engine.

DRIVER
Seated forward and left in the hull, the driver viewed the field with three M27 observation periscopes and an M24 infrared night scope. An aircraft-style wheel was used for steering. The brake and accelerator pedals were similar to those of an automobile.

With the advent of the M48 series medium tanks, the U.S. Army acquired the combat tank that was to become the mainstay of its armored fleet for decades. It remains in service with a number of armies around the world to this day.

M48A1 PATTON

M48A3 PATTON – SPECIFICATION

Country of Origin: USA
Crew: 4
Designer: Not specified
Designed: 1951–53
Manufacturer: Chrysler, Fisher Tank Arsenal, Ford Motor Company
In Production: 1952–59
Number Built: 12,000
In Service: 1950s–90s
Gross Weight: 51.7 tons (47 tonnes)

Dimensions:
Hull Length: 22.6 ft (6.82 m)
Length (gun forward): 24.4 ft (7.44 m)
Width: 11.9 ft (3.63 m)
Overall Height: 10.1 ft (3.1 m)

Performance:
Maximum Speed: 30 mph (48 km/h)
Range, Road: 290 miles (465 km)
Range, Cross-country: 180 miles (300 km)
Ground Pressure: 0.83 kg/cm^2
Fording Capacity: 4 ft (1.2 m)
Maximum Gradient: 30 degrees
Maximum Trench Width: 8.5 ft (2.6 m)
Maximum Vertical Obstacle: 3 ft (0.9 m)
Suspension Type: Torsion bar

Engine:
Powerplant: 1 x Continental AVDS-1790-2A supercharged V-12 diesel engine
Capacity: 6.5 gallons (29.4 l)
Output: 750 bhp/559 kW @ 2400 rpm

Power/Weight Ratio: 15.9 bhp/ton
Fuel Capacity: 312.1 gallons (1420 l)

Armament and Armor:
Main Armament: 1 x 3.5-in (90-mm) gun
Secondary Armament: 0.3-in (7.62-mm) machine gun
Ancillary Armament: 0.5-in (12.7-mm) machine gun
Armor Type: Homogenous cast/welded nickel-steel
Hull Front: 3.9–4.7 in (100–120 mm)
Hull Sides: 2–2.9 in (50–75 mm)
Hull Rear: 1.8 in (45 mm)
Hull Top: 2.2 in (57 mm)
Hull Bottom: 0.5–2.5 in (13–63 mm)
Turret Front: 4.3 in (110 mm)
Turret Sides: 2.9 in (75 mm)
Turret Rear: 2 in (50 mm)
Turret Top: 1 in (25 mm)

Major Variants:
M48: Differed from the M47 in having another new turret design and a redesigned hull.
M48A1: New driver hatch and M1 commander's cupola.
M48A2: Improved powerpack and transmission, redesigned rear plate, and improved turret control.
M48A3: Refit of M48A1s with diesel engines.
M48A3 Mod. B: Additional rear armor and raised commander's cupola.
M48A4: Proposed refit of M48A3s with M60 turrets, scrapped.
M48A5: Upgunned with the 4-in (105-mm) M68 gun.
M48A5PI: M1 cupola replaced by the Israeli Urdan model.
M67 "Zippo": M48 armed with a flamethrower inside a dummy model of the main gun with fake muzzle brake.

M47 PATTON

M48A3 PATTON

A modification of earlier variants of the M48 Patton medium tank, the M48A3 was delivered to the U.S. Army in early 1963 and subsequently deployed for service during the Vietnam War. The 810 hp (604 kW), V-12 Continental AVDS-1790-5B gas engine, which had been prone to catching fire, was replaced in the M48A3 with the 750 hp (560 kW) Continental AVDS-1790-2 diesel powerplant, which improved fuel consumption. The Allison CD-850-6A cross drive transmission was also installed. In 1967, additions to the M48A3 Mod. B included protective boxes covering the tail lights, more armor around the exhaust door louvres, and an adapter ring that raised the commander's cupola by 5 in (12.7 cm).

M48A5 PATTON

Manning his M48 Patton tank's turret-mounted 0.5-in (12.7-mm) machine gun, a commander scans the field and maintains communication with a headset while a crewman emerges from a second hatch. The tank's powerful searchlight is clearly visible.

The M48 has adapted well to improvement and modification, and is still used in large numbers. Because it is reliable, relatively cheap, and available in large quantities, many armies have decided to upgrade their M48s, rather than replace them.

The longevity of the M48, the third and final of the Patton series of tanks, has been remarkable. Named for General George S. Patton, commander of the U.S. Third Army during World War II, the Pattons were designed to battle Soviet-built tanks during the early Cold War period.

During the early 1950s, major modifications were made to the turret and hull of the existing M47 medium tank. The egg-shaped, sloping armor of the M48's turret, cast in a single piece of steel, offered enhanced ballistic protection, strength, and lighter weight, while reducing the angles more susceptible to enemy shells. The hull, with its bowl shape and further rounded edges, proved stronger than the previous box-like hull configuration and was also cast in a single piece. Additional armor plate was often welded to the exterior. The glacis was armored up to 4.7 in (120 mm) with a 60-degree slope.

The original gas engine had a bad reputation thanks to its tendency to ignite. A decade after the first M48 was delivered to the U.S. Army, the tank was fitted with a Continental diesel engine to rectify this. Other drawbacks included high fuel consumption and the absence of a stabilization system for the main 3.54-in (90-mm) M41 cannon, which made accurate fire on the move virtually impossible. Secondary armament consisted of a 0.5-in (12.7-mm) turret-mounted machine gun, and a coaxial 0.3-in (7.62-mm) machine gun.

CONTINUOUSLY IMPROVING TECHNOLOGY

Significant technological advances were incorporated into the M48, including a fully enclosed machine-gun mount on the commander's cupola with the M48A1, larger fuel tanks, better fire control, a T-shaped muzzle brake, and a fuel-injected engine with the M48A2, and the installation of the diesel engine. The commander's cupola was raised, and a simplified rangefinder was fitted on the M48A3, of which 1019 were built. The first 600 went to the U.S. Army and the remainder went to the U.S. Marine Corps. Highly sophisticated for its time, the fire-control system of the

M48A3 was comprised of a series of mirrors and a ballistic computer that was operated with cams and gears.

Variants of the M48 were manufactured by the Fisher Tank Arsenal, Chrysler Corporation, and Ford Motor Company, while the modifications of the earlier models to the M48A3 were completed at the army's Anniston and Red River depots. These modifications further included a carbon dioxide fire-extinguishing system and equipment for chemical, biological, and radiologic warfare. Other variations to the M48A1 resulted in the M48A3 Mod B, with the raised cupola and protection for running lights.

The Israeli Defense Force initiated an upgrade of more than 600 M48s beginning in the mid-1960s, improving the standard main armament from 3.54 in (90 mm) to the 4-in (105-mm) L7A1, enhancing the fire-control system, and reducing the cupola profile. The Americans picked up these modifications, designating the improved tanks as M48A5. More than 600 M48s were deployed during the Vietnam War, while the tank was also in action during the Indo-Pakistani wars of 1965 and 1971, and during the Six-Day War of 1967. Thousands of M48s remain in service today.

Close-up

The M48A3 Patton tank has experienced a lengthy service life due to its adaptability and ease of upgrade. Numerous nations have chosen to enhance their standard M48s with more recent systems.

1. **Commander's Cupola:** The M48 commander was positioned on the left inside the turret.

2. **Searchlight:** The xenon searchlight, sighted with both the main 3.5-in (90-mm) weapon and gunsights, was capable of operating in standard or infrared modes.

3. **Turret:** The elliptical shape of the turret was a departure from previous designs and facilitated fighting in the hull-down position.

4. **Main Armament:** The 3.54-in (90-mm) M41 main cannon was mounted in a slightly redesigned turret on the M48A3 Patton tank.

5. **Sloped Armor:** The 60-degree slope of the glacis armor on the upper hull of the M48A3 effectively increased its thickness and the protection afforded the crew.

6. **Lower Hull:** This was cast in a single piece, with additional armor plating often welded on to protect against anti-tank mines.

M41 Walker Bulldog

Implementing lessons learned in combat during World War II, U.S. engineers developed the M41 Walker Bulldog. This light, air-transportable tank was armed well enough to defend itself and was compatible with parts designed for other armored vehicles.

INTERNAL CONFIGURATION

Divided into three compartments, with the driver to the front, the fighting compartment at center, and the engine compartment separated by a firewall to the rear, the M41 interior was highly functional, though American crews complained of limited headroom.

TURRET

The cast and welded turret of the M41 was distinguished by its elongated bustle. It accommodated three crewmen.

DRIVER

The M41 driver sat forwards and to the left in the hull. A drop-out escape hatch was provided through the floor of the hull under the driver's seat.

FACTS

- Intended to be air-transportable, the M41 eventually became too heavy for airlift deployment.
- The Brazilian armed forces upgunned the M41 with a 3.54-in (90-mm) cannon.
- The M41 was named the Walker Bulldog for General Walton H. Walker, who died in a jeep accident in Korea in 1950.

MAIN ARMAMENT
The 3-in (76-mm) M32 main cannon featured an automatic loader, the first to be installed in a U.S.-manufactured tank. The loader was used to select, lift, index, and ram the shell into position, and then to dispense of the empty casings.

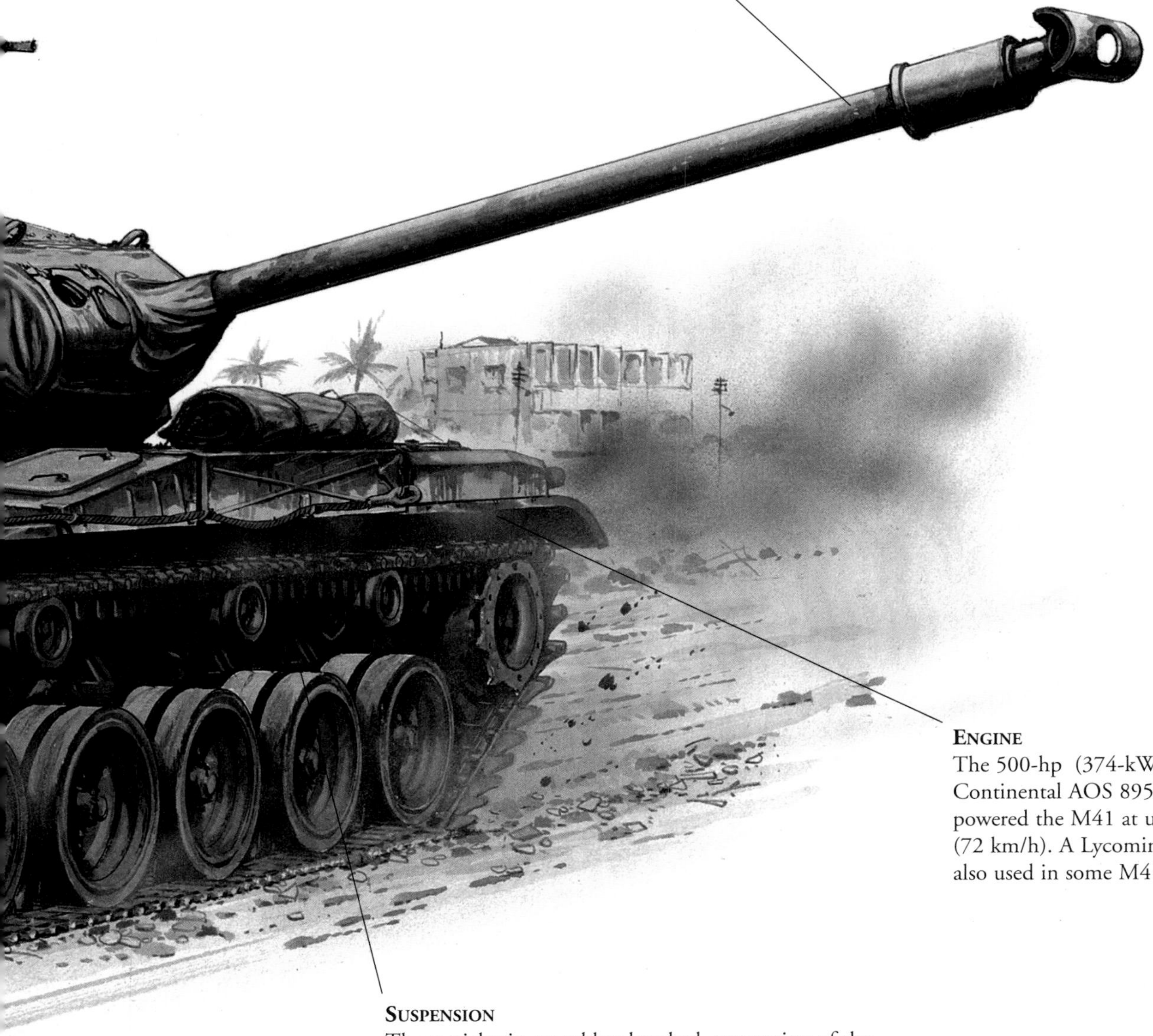

ENGINE
The 500-hp (374-kW), six-cylinder Continental AOS 895-3 engine powered the M41 at up to 45 mph (72 km/h). A Lycoming engine was also used in some M41s.

SUSPENSION
The torsialastic, or rubber-brushed, suspension of the M41 included torsion bars and hydraulic shock absorbers. The drive sprocket was positioned at the rear, with an idler to the front and three return rollers, providing a relatively smooth cross-country ride.

The T41E1, which became the M41, was fitted with a state-of-the-art power train. This was interchangeable with components in several other vehicles in the army's tactical fleet. Its clean and efficient design made the tank a worthy successor to the M24.

M41 WALKER BULLDOG – SPECIFICATION

Country of Origin: USA
Crew: 4
Designer: Not specified
Designed: Late 1940s
Manufacturer: Cadillac
In Production: 1951–69
In Service: 1953–present
Number Built: 2100
Weight: 25.9 tons (23.5 tonnes)

Dimensions:
Hull Length: 19.1 ft (5.8 m)
Length, gun forward: 27 ft (8.2 m)
Width: 10.5 ft (3.2 m)
Height: 8.9 ft (2.71 m)

Performance:
Speed: 45 mph (72 km/h)
Range, Road: 140 miles (225 km)
Range, Cross-country: 60 miles (100 km)
Ground Pressure: 0.72 kg/cm²
Fording Capacity: 3.3 ft (1.1 m)
Maximum Gradient: 31 degrees
Maximum Trench Width: 6 ft (1.8 m)
Maximum Vertical Obstacle: 2.3 ft (0.7 m)

Engine:
Powerplant: 1 x Continental AOS 895-3 6-cylinder gas 500-hp (374-kW) engine
Capacity: 3.88 gallons (14.7 l)
Power/Weight Ratio: 21.3 hp/ton
Suspension: Torsion bar

Armament and Armor:
Primary Armament: 1 x 3-in (76-mm) L/52 M32 gun
Secondary Armament: 1 x 0.3-in (7.69-mm) Browning M1919A4E1 machine gun
Ancillary Armament: 1 x 0.5-in (12.7-mm) Browning M2 HB AA machine gun
Armor Type: Homogenous nickel-steel rolled/welded hull, cast/welded turret
Hull Front: 1–1.3 in (25–32 mm)
Hull Sides: 0.75–1 in (19–25 mm)
Hull Rear: 0.75 in (19 mm)
Hull Top: 0.47–0.59 in (12–15 mm)
Hull Bottom: 0.35–1.3 in (9–32 mm)
Turret Front: 1 in (25 mm)
Turret Sides: 1 in (25 mm)
Turret Rear: 1 in (25 mm)
Turret Top: 0.51 in (13 mm)

Variants:
M41A1: (1953) Hydraulic instead of electrical turret traverse.
M41A2: (1956) Production tanks with fuel-injected Continental 6-cylinder gas engine replacing carburetor fuel system.
M41A3: M41A1 tanks with engines upgraded to fuel injection.
M41 DK-1: Danish upgrade. New engine, thermal sights.
Type 64 (Experimental): Taiwanese development modified. Did not enter mass production and is not to be confused with another M42-based light tank conversion bearing the same designation.
M41D: Taiwanese upgrade.
M42 Duster: (1952) Self-propelled anti-aircraft defense weapon system based on the M41 chassis.

M41 WALKER BULLDOG

The successor to the M24 Chaffee light tank, which was deployed late in 1944 and saw only limited service during World War II, the M41 Walker Bulldog continued to be built on a theme of compatibility among a team of armored vehicles capable of utilizing the same chassis and common components. The rangefinder, fully enclosed in the cast and welded turret, proved troublesome and delayed production until 1951. While the driver was situated in the hull, the three crew members in the turret were sometimes hampered by limited space. Both commander and loader had access to hatches, which opened to the rear.

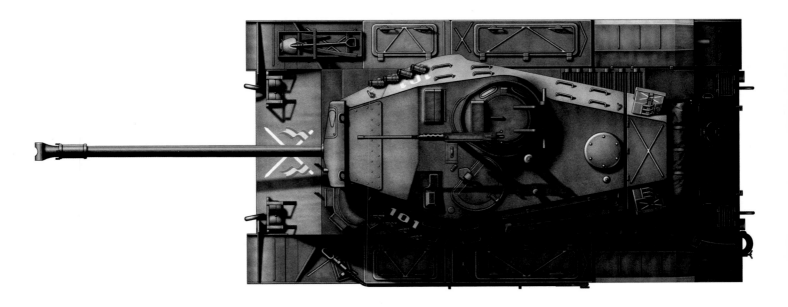

Pausing along a street in a South Vietnamese city, the American crewmen of a Walker Bulldog tank watch traffic move past as infantrymen maintain a continuing cordon of security against Viet Cong infiltrators.

The M41 Walker Bulldog was developed as a fast, agile light tank for close infantry support and cavalry reconnaissance. Carrying a 3-in (76-mm) M32 main gun, it was amply armed to defend itself even against enemy medium tanks.

In the wake of World War II, the U.S. Army was confronted with countering the perceived menace of communism on a global scale. American tank designers had already begun to heed the lessons of armored warfare gleaned from the battlefields of Europe. Applying these to their own designs and maintaining some adherence to the early U.S. armored doctrine of infantry support and scouting functions, the M41 Walker Bulldog emerged as the first post-war U.S. light tank to see extensive service around the world.

A relative few of the M41's predecessor, the M24 Chaffee, had seen action during World War II, and although the M24 design appeared to be solid and functional, the U.S. effort to upgrade continued. By 1949, the prototype T41E1 had largely been designed around the proposed powerplant, the 500-hp (374-kW), six-cylinder Continental AOS 895-3 or a comparable Lycoming engine, which had originally been intended for use in aircraft.

In response to the defense demands placed on the U.S. Army, the M41 – named the Walker Bulldog in honor of

General Walton H. Walker, who was killed in Korea in 1950 – was intended for rapid deployment, by air if necessary. It was meant to pack enough punch with its 3-in (76-mm) cannon to defend itself against heavier enemy tanks. Its armored protection ranged from 0.38–1.5 in (9.75 to 38 mm). Its secondary armament was a single hull-mounted Browning 0.3-in (7.62-mm) machine gun and a turret-mounted 0.5-in (12.7-mm) machine gun for anti-aircraft defense.

In the event, at 25.9 tons (23.5 tonnes), the M41 proved too heavy for reasonable air deployment. However, its firepower, top road speed of 45 mph (72 km/h), and range of 140 miles (225 km) proved to be valuable assets. Production began in 1951 at the Cleveland, Ohio, plant operated by the Cadillac division of General Motors, and 1802 were built.

COMPONENTS AND COMBAT

The M41 utilized a CD 500-3 cross-drive transmission with hydraulic torque converters, two forwards speeds, and a single reverse gear. Its innovative suspension included a combination of torsion bars and hydraulic shock absorbers. An automatic loader improved the 3-in (76-mm) cannon's rate of fire significantly, and the original rangefinder was replaced with a simplified version in production models. Infrared optics and searchlights facilitated nocturnal operations. The M41 was capable of fording just over 40 in (1 m) of still water and climbing a 30-in (76-cm) vertical obstruction. An external telephone was mounted in the hull for communication with infantry.

Even though it was deployed only on a limited basis during the Korean War, the tank was still designated T41. Its single greatest limitation was turret space, with limited headroom for three crewmen, yet the tank was deployed in significant numbers during the Vietnam War, becoming popular among South Vietnamese tank crews, generally of slighter stature than their American allies.

MULTI-NATIONAL USERS

The armed forces of more than 20 nations deployed the M41, and its combat record in Southeast Asia included the first armored engagement of the Vietnam War. During this incident three of five M41s, along with 25 armored personnel carriers, were lost. In addition, the South Vietnamese armored force and supporting air strikes destroyed 22 Soviet-built T-54 and PT-76 tanks.

Interior view

The cramped interior of the M41 made it a relatively unpopular vehicle with American armored crews. South Vietnamese soldiers who used the tank found the space to be adequate.

1. **Ballistic Unit:** This included a control knob for choosing the right type of ammunition to engage a selected target.

2. **Gun Breech:** The breech of the M41 Walker Bulldog's 3-in (76-mm) main gun was semi-automatic and installed vertically. A bin for spent shell casings was located nearby.

3. **Traverse Mechanism Hand Wheel:** This connected to the commander's hand control through a long crossrod, which ran towards the rear of the turret.

4. **Optics:** The M20 periscope and M79 telescope were the gunner's primary and back-up equipment for sighting targets for the pulsed relay system of the main weapon.

5. **Gun Firing Control Box:** This served as an electric switch panel, powering components of the 3-in (76-mm) gun-laying system.

6. **Gunner's Position:** The gunner was positioned to use the optics and manipulate manual hydraulic equipment to elevate the main weapon.

AMX-13

An early post–World War II French tank design, the AMX-13 was a light, air-mobile fighting vehicle. Its designers were responsible for introducing such innovations as an automatic loading system and oscillating turret. Variants have been exported to at least 25 countries.

TURRET
The oscillating turret of the AMX-13 involves a fixed main weapon while the upper half of the turret pivots on the lower half to change the gun's elevation.

LOADING SYSTEM
The main cannon was loaded with an automatic system of revolver-type magazines, two of which were available and held six shells apiece. After these two magazines were fired, the magazines were refilled manually.

AMMUNITION STORAGE
Because of space constraints and for reasons of safety, ammunition was regularly stored externally.

ENGINE
The 250-hp (187-kW) SOFAM 8Gxb eight-cylinder gas engine ran the length of the right side of the AMX-13 hull.

SECONDARY ARMAMENT
In various configurations, the secondary armament of the AMX-13 included a coaxial 0.29-in (7.5-mm) or 0.3-in (7.62-mm) machine gun on the right side of the main cannon and a 0.3-in (7.62-mm) anti-aircraft machine gun.

MAIN ARMAMENT
Originally armed with a 2.95-in (75-mm) cannon patterned after the World War II–vintage German 2.95-in (75-mm) KwK 42 L/70 mounted on the PzKpfw V Panther medium tank, the AMX-13 was upgunned to a 3.54-in (90-mm) weapon and then a 4-in (105-mm) for export.

FACTS

- Production of AMX-13 variants lasted from 1952–87.

- Approximately half of the 7700 AMX-13 variants were exported.

- Early gas engines were retrofitted with diesel powerplants to minimize the risk of fire and improve range.

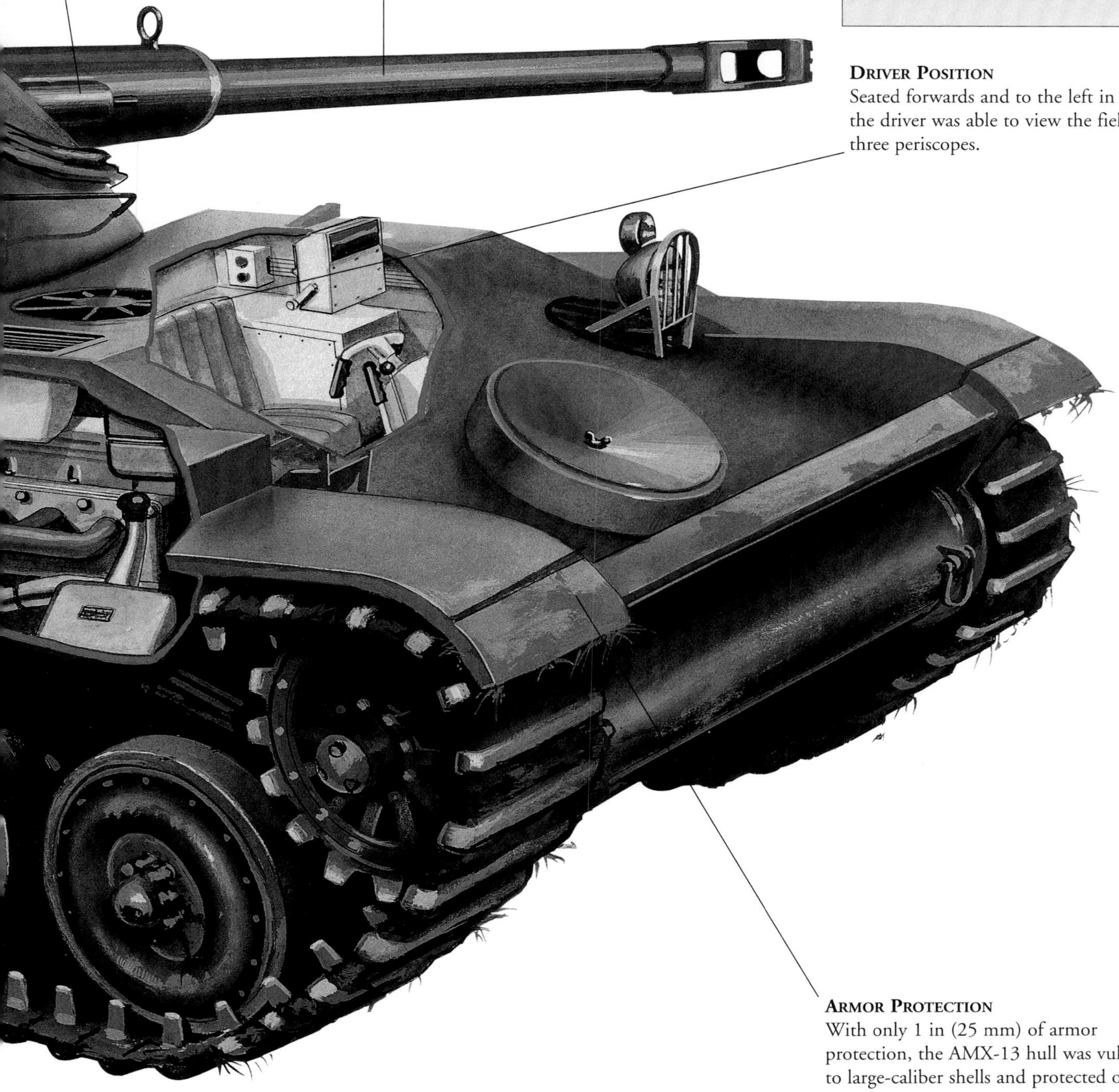

DRIVER POSITION
Seated forwards and to the left in the hull, the driver was able to view the field through three periscopes.

ARMOR PROTECTION
With only 1 in (25 mm) of armor protection, the AMX-13 hull was vulnerable to large-caliber shells and protected only against small arms, splinters, and flash burn.

In 1946, when work on the design of the AMX-13 began, the tank was intended to be used as a tank destroyer and reconnaissance vehicle. As the tank developed, the manufacturer, Atelier de Construction Roanne (ARE), modified the design slightly and produced a true light tank.

AMX-13

AMX-13 – SPECIFICATION

Country of Origin: France
Crew: 3
Designer: Atelier de Construction d'Issy-les-Moulineaux
Designed: 1946
In Production: 1952–87
Manufacturer: Atelier de Construction Roanne
In Service: 1953–present
Number Built: 7700
Gross Weight: 16.5 tons (15 tonnes)

Dimensions:
Hull Length: 16 ft (4.88 m)
Length (gun forward): 20.9 ft (6.36 m)
Width: 8.2 ft (2.5 m)
Overall Height: 7.6 ft (2.3 m) (to cupola top)

Performance:
Maximum Speed: 37 mph (60 km/h)
Range, Road: 250 miles (400 km)
Range, Cross-country: 150 miles (250 km)
Ground Pressure: 0.76 kg/cm²
Fording Capacity: 2 ft (0.6 m)
Maximum Gradient: 30 degrees
Maximum Trench Width: 5.25 ft (1.6 m)
Maximum Vertical Obstacle: 2.2 ft (0.65 m)
Suspension Type: Torsion bars

Engine:
Powerplant: 1 x SOFAM (Saviem) 8GXb V-8 liquid-cooled gas
Capacity: n/a
Output: 250 hp (187 kW) @ 3200 rpm
Power/Weight Ratio: 16.7 bhp/ton
Fuel Capacity: 106 gallons (480 l)

Armor and Armament:
Main Armament: 1 x 2.95-in (75-mm) L/57 (1967 replaced by 3.54 in [90 mm])
Secondary Armament: 2 x 0.29-in (7.5-mm) or 0.3-in (7.62-mm) FN1/AAT52 machine guns
Armor Type: Homogeneous rolled/welded nickel-steel with cast turret
Hull Front: 1.58 in (40 mm)
Hull Sides: 0.79 in (20 mm)
Hull Rear: 0.59 in (15 mm)
Hull Top: 0.39 in (10 mm)
Hull Bottom: 0.39 in (10 mm)
Turret Front: 1.58 in (40 mm)
Turret Sides: 0.79 in (20 mm)
Turret Rear: 0.79 in (20 mm)
Turret Top: 0.39 in (10 mm)

Variants:
75 Modèle 51: High-velocity 2.95-in (75-mm) gun in FL-11 turret.
T75 (Char Lance SS-11): Fitted with SS-11 ATGM launchers.
T75 avec TCA: Fitted with electronic missile guidance system.
90 Modèle 52: FL-10 turret refitted with F3 3.54-in (90-mm) gun.
90 LRF: Fitted with laser rangefinder.
105 Modèle 58: Fitted with 4-in (105-mm) gun in FL-12 turret.
13/105: Upgraded export version of the Modele 58.
Model 1987: Late production version.
DCA aka AMX-13/S530: SPAAG version.
DCA 30: (aka Bitube de 1.18-in [30-mm] anti-aérien automoteur, Oeil Noir) SPAAG version with retractable radar.
[Training Tank]: AMX-13 with turret removed.
Modèle 55 (AMX-D): Recovery version.
PDP (Poseur De Pont) Modèle 51: Scissors-type bridgelayer.

VARIANT: AMX-13 DCA ANTI-AIRCRAFT

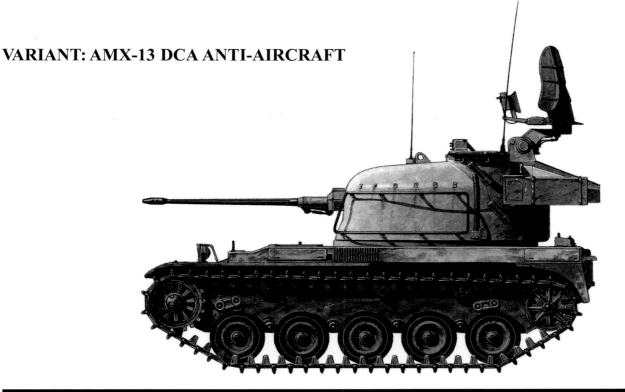

AMX-13

The interior of the AMX-13 was divided into a forward compartment holding the engine on the right and running the length of the hull, and the driver on the left, along with a fighting compartment accommodating the commander and gunner to the rear. The oscillating turret was fitted towards the rear of the chassis and featured an automatic loading system, which fired six-round magazines. One of the driver's viewing periscopes was often retrofitted with an infrared scope for night vision, while the commander was situated under a domed cupola with 360-degree visibility. Early optics were improved with computers and laser rangefinders.

SUPPORT VEHICLE: PANHARD EBR ARMORED CAR

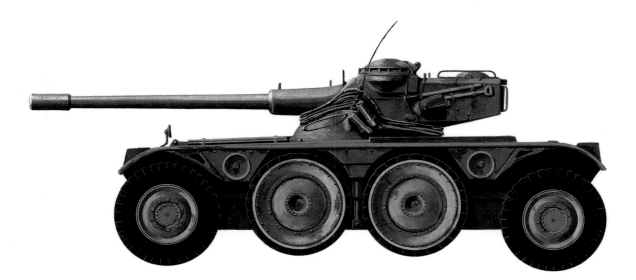

Even though it is now functionally obsolescent, the AMX-13 remains in service with several countries. The Israeli army used the tank in its 1956 and 1967 wars, but found it unsatisfactory. It was phased out of service with the French army in the 1970s.

The innovations of the French-built AMX-13 light tank proved modern in concept but troublesome at times in application. Conceived in the wake of World War II, the tank was named in recognition of its original weight, 14 tons (13 tonnes). Later versions, carrying heavier armament and diesel engines, weighed 16.5 tons (15 tonnes) or more. Intended as a fire support and reconnaissance vehicle for airborne troops, it was deployable by air. However, its air mobile weight was achieved at the expense of adequate armor protection (0.98 in [25 mm]), making the vehicle vulnerable to virtually any anti-tank weapon in service.

Close-up

The AMX-13 was innovative in concept and design, but it proved a disappointment under the rigors of combat. Nevertheless, it was a popular export to other nations, and was produced for 25 years.

(1) **Main Weapon System:** Early AMX-13s were armed with a 2.9-in (75-mm) cannon, but were upgraded to 4 in (105 mm).

(2) **Light Weight:** The tank's light weight made it air-transportable to fulfill its primary role of fire support and reconnaissance for airborne troops.

(3) **Driver Position:** The driver sat in the front of the hull and to the left, with the engine running the length of the right side.

(4) **Oscillating Turret:** Along with an automatic loading system for the main weapon, the oscillating turret was also an innovation.

(5) **Smoke Grenade Launcher:** External smoke grenade launchers were commonly used to provide concealment for the vehicle and infantry units in Cold War era tanks.

(6) **Ammunition Storage:** This was outside the tank, which meant reloading was somewhat problematic.

One of the more than 100 variants of the French AMX-13 light tank rolls down a thoroughfare during parade activities. The AMX-13 was light and maneuverable, though limited armor protection made it highly vulnerable to enemy fire.

Further, the AMX-13 introduced a Fives-Gail Babcock oscillating turret, which included a fixed main gun on the upper half of the turret. Pivoting the upper half of the turret on the lower half raised or lowered the main gun's elevation. In certain mountainous terrain, the turret rendered the main gun almost unusable. Although such a turret configuration facilitated the introduction of an automatic loading system, eliminating the need for a fourth crewman, the loading system fired only two six-round magazines. Once these initial 12 shells were fired, the weapon had to be served manually because the magazines were reloaded outside the vehicle. This stretched the effectiveness of the three-man crew heavily in combat, and put them at further risk.

ARMS FOR SALE

Early AMX-13 models were powered by the eight-cylinder SOFAM 8Gxb gas engine generating 250 hp (187 kW). However, some countries have opted for diesel engines to reduce the potential for fire and increase the vehicle's range. The original turret, designated the FL-10, mounted the German-inspired 2.95-in (75-mm) cannon with a single baffle muzzle brake based on that of the Panther medium tank of World War II. It fired at a rate of one round every five seconds until its magazines were emptied.

By 1966, the 3.54-in (90-mm) AMX-13/90 gun had been introduced in the new FL-12 turret, and many existing tanks were retrofitted with the improved weapon. Along with secondary armament of a 0.29-in (7.5-mm) or 0.3-in (7.62-mm) coaxial machine gun and a 0.3-in (7.62-mm) anti-aircraft machine gun, a third light machine gun could be mounted near the commander's cupola for added infantry support. The original torsion bar suspension was upgraded with a hydro-pneumatic system in 1985 along with the introduction of a fully automatic transmission and a standard diesel engine.

Production of the AMX-13 began at ARE in 1952 following at least five years of research and development and was taken over by Cruesot-Loire in 1964. By the time production ceased in 1987, more than 7700 had been built. Over 3000 of these were exported from France to other countries, and a version specifically for export had been upgunned with a low-velocity 4-in (105-mm) cannon. A number of purchasers improved their AMX-13s with better weapons or added nuclear, biological, and chemical defensive systems along with night fighting technology.

More than 100 variants of the AMX-13 have been developed during five decades of service. These include an armored personnel carrier and platforms for self-propelled artillery and anti-tank guided missile systems.

M60

The initial U.S. main battle tank of the Cold War era, the M60 can be categorized as the fourth incarnation of the post-war Patton series or considered a direct descendant. First developed in response to the improvements made in Soviet armor, the M60 remains in service today.

SECONDARY ARMAMENT
A 0.5-in (12.7-mm) M2 heavy machine gun mounted on the commander's cupola was complemented by at least one 0.3-in (7.62-mm) coaxial machine gun and sometimes a second near the loader's hatch. On each side of the turret, a six-round smoke grenade launcher was attached.

TURRET
The original M60 turret was similar to that of the M48, being elliptical in shape. However, the A1 and A3 variants mounted a needle-nose turret, which presented a reduced frontal area in combat.

INTERIOR CONFIGURATION
As with the Patton series, the M60 was divided into three compartments: the fighting compartment in the center, engine and transmission compartment to the rear, and the driver compartment to the front.

FACTS

- First deployed in 1960, the M60 served with Coalition forces during Operation Desert Storm.
- A powerful searchlight, capable of white and infrared, was installed on the M60A1 but removed from many M60A3s.
- The M60A2 "Starship" incorporated leading-edge technology but proved to be a disappointment.

Main Armament
The 4-in (105-mm) M68, a license-built version of the British L7A1 cannon, was installed on the M60 and on the tanks of several other countries.

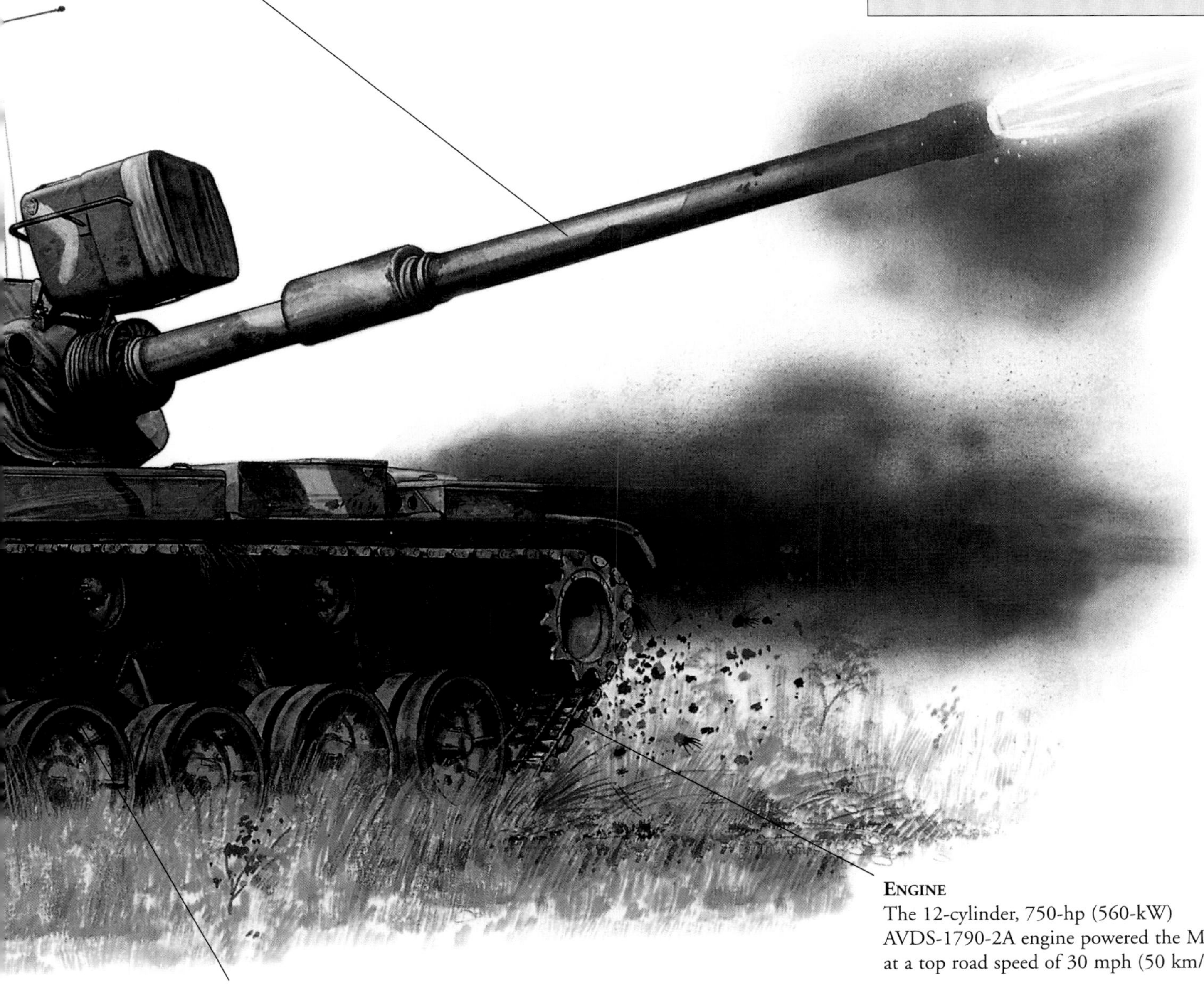

Engine
The 12-cylinder, 750-hp (560-kW) AVDS-1790-2A engine powered the M60 at a top road speed of 30 mph (50 km/h).

Suspension
A torsion bar suspension was installed in more than one design in the M60 series. This included the tube over bar system, in which the torsion bar was enclosed in a tube, connected together at one end, and worked as a double suspension.

An external layer of appliqué armor was fitted to some M60A3s to give the tank adequate protection against the improved weapons systems it would encounter in the 1990s. The extra protection centered on the turret and the front glacis plate.

M60

M60

Placed in production in 1977, the M60A3 weighed 57 tons (52 tonnes), nearly the same as the M60A1, but incorporated a number of improvements over the earlier model, including a Hughes integrated laser rangefinding sight and thermal night sight for the commander, a VGS-2 thermal imaging sight and Hughes VVG-2 laser rangefinder for the gunner, and a solid-state ballistic computer with increased accuracy and an operating range of 656 ft–5500 yards (200–5000 m). A previous improvement to the original M60 design moved the main gun forward 5 in (12 cm), providing additional space inside the three-man turret. An Israeli-designed HALON automatic fire extinguisher system was standard on the M60A3.

VARIANT: M728 CEV

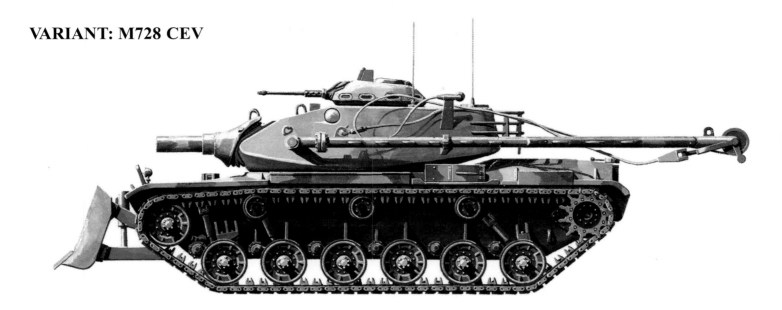

M60 – SPECIFICATION

Country of Origin: USA
Crew: 4
Designer: Not specified
Designed: 1957–59
Manufacturer: Detroit Arsenal Tank Plant, Chrysler
In Production: 1959–83
In Service: 1960–97
Numbers Built: More than 15,000
Weight: 50.7 tons (46 tonnes)

Dimensions:
Length: 22 ft 9 in (6.94 m)
Width: 11 ft (3.6 m)
Height: 10 ft 6 in (3.2 m)

Performance:
Speed: 30 mph (48 km/h)
Operational range: 300 miles (480 km)

Engine:
Powerplant: 1 x Continental AVDS-1790-2 V12, air-cooled
twin-turbo diesel engine 750 hp (560 kW)
Power/weight Ratio: 14.5 hp/ton
Suspension: Torsion bar suspension
Ground clearance: 15.3 in (389 mm)

Armor and Armament:
Armor: 5.9 in (150 mm)
Main armament: 1 x 4.1-in (105-mm) M68 gun (M60/A1/A3);
1 x 6-in (152-mm) M162 Gun/Launcher (M60A2)
Secondary armament: 1 x 0.50-in (12.7-mm) M85;
1 x 0.3-in (7.62-mm) machine gun

Variants:
XM60/M60: Bearing a strong resemblance to the M48, the
M60 also has a wedge-shaped hull, three return rollers, and
aluminium road wheels. Early versions did not have the
commander's cupola.
M60A1: First variant to feature the distinctive needle-nose turret.
M60A1 AOS: Add-On Stabilization introduced in 1972 for the
M68 gun.
M60A1 RISE: Reliability Improvements for Selected Equipment,
featured improvements of almost all the basic systems,
including an upgraded engine design that enabled easier
access to components to allow removing the engine pack in
less time.
M60A1 RISE Passive: RISE, but with a smaller infrared/white
light-capable searchlight and passive night vision equipment.
M60A1E1: Developmental test vehicles fitted with the 6-in (152-
mm) M162 gun-missile launchers.
M60A1E2/M60A2: Turret design finalized, giving the
distinctive "starship" look. A variant was tested with a remote-
controlled 0.79-in (20-mm) cannon as well.
M60A1E3: Prototype M60A1E2 fitted with 4.1-in (105-mm) gun.
M60A1E4: Experimental type with remote-control weapons.
M60A3: M60A1 fitted with a laser rangefinder.
M60A3 TTS: M60A3s fitted with the AN/VSG-2 thermal sight.
M60 Super/AX: Uparmored versions with minor improvements.
M60-2000/120S: M60/Abrams hybrid vehicle developed by
General Dynamics Land Division. Not adopted by the United
States military.
M728 CEV: M60A1-based Combat Engineer Vehicle.
M728A1: Upgraded version of the M728 CEV.

In 1956, intelligence reports regarding tank development in the Soviet Union suggested that a tank more capable than the T-54/T-55 main battle tank was being developed. A design team suggested that there was plenty of room for improving the M48, and upgrade programs were immediately undertaken.

Production of the M60 main battle tank began at the height of the Cold War. It was based largely on the M48, even though the older design was considered inferior to a coming generation of improved Soviet tanks. The M48 was hampered in combat by its short range and extreme fuel consumption, heavy weight, and comparatively thin armor protection. The improved M60 entered service in 1960 and comprised the bulk of U.S. fighting armor for the next 20 years. Eventually the M1 Abrams largely replaced it, yet production of the M60 did not cease until 1987. Altogether, more than 15,000 M60s were manufactured.

Interior view

The M60 was designed as the first U.S. main battle tank of the Cold War era and is one of the world's most successful main battle tanks, with 15,000 having been produced.

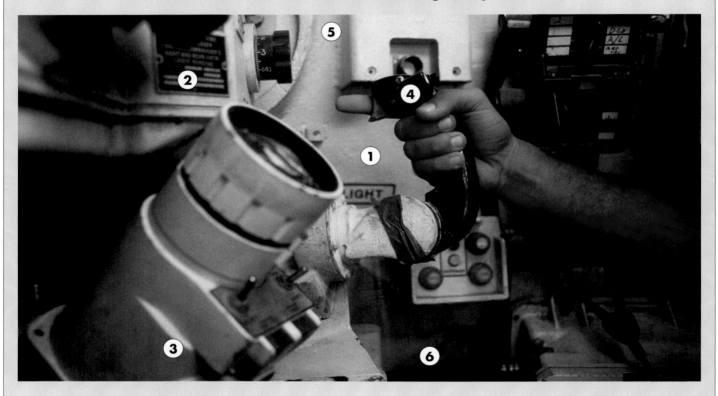

(1) **Commander's Position:** The commander sat in the turret above the gunner. The turret-mounted machine gun fired from the cupola.

(2) **Laser Rangefinder:** The laser rangefinder emits a laser beam that indentifies the target and provides a range, or distance, to the target for the main weapon to fire at.

(3) **4-in (105-mm) Night Sight:** The tank commander's night sight is an extension of the gunner's, enabling him to see what the gunner sees at night or during the day.

(4) **Tank Commander Override:** This allows the commander to elevate, depress, and fire the main cannon, traverse the turret, and follow moving targets.

(5) **Lighting:** The night sight uses ambient light rather than thermal imaging, as does the main gun's night sight.

(6) **Turret Basket:** The turret basket rotates in concert as the turret traverses, allowing the crew to orient themselves immediately to the interior of the M60 tank.

The externally-mounted laser rangefinder and smoke grenade launchers are affixed to the turret of the M60 main battle tank. Note the large searchlight, commander's cupola, and driver positioned in the center of the hull.

The turret of the original M60 was subsequently replaced in the M60A1 and A3 models as designers opted for a cast needle-nose configuration, which offered a minimal target and improved armor protection in excess of 5 in (127 mm). The commander, gunner, and loader were positioned in the M60 turret, with the gunner in front and on the right, the loader above and to the left, and the commander directly behind and above the gunner. Seated in the left front of the hull and protected by armor up to 5.9 in (150 mm) thick, the driver viewed the surrounding terrain through three periscopes and an infrared scope for night vision. Both the commander and the gunner had good fields of vision. The gunner used a roof-mounted periscope, which could be interchanged with an infrared version, while the commander used eight vision slits circuiting the hand-rotated cupola.

THE "STARSHIP" DISAPPOINTS

The heavy 4-in (105-mm) M68 cannon could be ranged and fired by either the gunner or the commander, both of whom could also traverse the turret. The license-built M68 was a British design, which also equipped the tanks of several other nations, including the German Leopard I and later production models of the British Centurion.

The M60A2 variant was a radical departure from the main battle tank standard and proved to be a disappointment.

Nicknamed the "Starship," the M60A2 incorporated a redesigned turret mounting the Shillelagh weapons system, which proved unreliable. The Shillelagh weighed about half as much as a more conventional main gun, and the complicated 6-in (152-mm) system was capable of firing missiles or conventional high explosive, white phosphorus, or training ammunition rounds. Fewer than 550 of the M60A2 were built, and these were soon placed in storage.

By 1977, the production of the M60A3 and the upgrading of many M60A1 models already in service had begun. Beyond the improved fire control installed on the M60A3, a better track system, with pads that could be replaced by the crewmen, were added. The M60A3 was also given smokescreen capability, along with a snorkel, which allowed the tank to ford water to a depth of almost 13 ft (4 m).

A relative few M60s were deployed to Vietnam, and the tanks entered combat with the Israeli Defense Force during the Yom Kippur War. They were also used during the Iran-Iraq War and in Operation Desert Storm. Reviews of the performance of early M60s were mixed, particulary when confronted with the Soviet Sagger anti-tank missile. However, modifications allowed the M60 to keep pace with the latest in Soviet armor during its tenure. Today, numerous countries continue to field the M60, and the process of upgrading the design goes on.

Modern Tanks 1961–Present

Continuing implementation of rapidly advancing technology has brought about a refinement of the capabilities of the tank. From unprecedented firepower to equipment that pierces the dark of night, tanks and armored fighting vehicles have transformed the modern battlefield.

The British Challenger II main battle tank was initially armed with the 4.7-in (120-mm) L30 rifled gun. Its innovative design incorporated few of the components of its Challenger I predecessor.

The awesome, deadly firepower of the U.S. 24th Infantry Division, which included more than 200 M1A1 Abrams main battle tanks, electrified the world as its forces stalked and destroyed elements of the Iraqi Republican Guard during Operation Desert Storm. A host of Coalition armor, including the British Challenger, the French AMX-30, and others, demonstrated the ability of the main battle tank to dominate a hostile landscape.

Opposing the Coalition forces, the Iraqi army had employed primarily export variants of the Soviet-manufactured T-54/55, T-62, and T-72 tanks. Capable when maintained for peak performance or provided with the updated technology necessary to survive on the modern battlefield, the Iraqi armor may indeed have been degraded and at a disadvantage from the beginning. One common thread for both sides, however, is the lineage of these beasts of battle, weighing in excess of 50 tons (49 tonnes) and mounting main weapons of 4.7 in (120 mm) or greater.

DIVISION OF LABOR

At the height of the Cold War, the strategic arms race made headlines as a doctrine of "mutually assured destruction" with nuclear-armed intercontinental ballistic missiles weighed on the collective psyche. At the same time, however, the tank, which would be put to the tactical test in the event of a conventional war, was steadily upgraded. While weaponry was improved, gun platforms were stabilized, fire control was upgraded with infrared sensors and thermal imaging, a new generation of composite armor provided unprecedented protection, computers became capable of tracking multiple targets simultaneously, and defenses against nuclear, biological, and chemical weapons were developed.

Meanwhile, the role of the tank as a light, medium, or heavy armored vehicle, deployed for scout and reconnaissance missions, tank-versus-tank combat, or long-range fire support, was evaluated by designers and military theorists both East and West. Through trial and error, tinkering and testing, the concept of the main battle tank, capable of a variety of missions, was born. The Soviet T-64 and later variants, the British Chieftain and Challenger, the French AMX-30, the Israeli Merkava, the German Leopard, and the tanks of the U.S. Patton series and its successor the Abrams embodied the traditional advantages of the tank – firepower, armor protection, and mobility – while serving as platforms for the latest in military technology.

The M2/M3 Bradley fighting vehicle overcame scandal and difficulties during more than 15 years of development to perform exceptionally well throughout deployments to the Middle East and the Balkans.

RAGE AGAINST THE MACHINE

As the prowess of the main battle tank progressed, the defenses against it grew more sophisticated as well. Combat conditions revealed shortcomings in certain areas, and while these were exploited by adversaries, they were being addressed by engineers and designers. Given the challenges of difficult terrain, the jungles of Southeast Asia provided a stern test for the deployment of tanks and armored vehicles against an insurgency and a well-armed and organized enemy. U.S. tanks and armored personnel carriers regularly faced a gauntlet of rocket-propelled grenades, particularly the Soviet RPG-7, and anti-tank mines buried along roadways.

During the Yom Kippur War, Israeli tanks, which had performed tremendously during the Six-Day War of 1967, were devastated by squads of Egyptian infantrymen with the portable Soviet-made AT-3 Sagger anti-tank missile. The U.S. developed the LAW (Light Anti-tank Weapon) and the TOW, a wire-guided missile system fired from a platform such as a jeep or armored personnel carrier. As tank technology improved, the ability to destroy or disable the tank gained greater importance, and a continual contest of technological one-upmanship ensued.

URBAN AND OPEN COUNTRY

While armored encounters such as those of the Indo-Pakistani wars, the modern wars of the Arab-Israeli conflict, the major battles of the Gulf War, and the 2003 invasion of Iraq have demonstrated the awesome power of the tank, low-intensity conflict has tested the ability of the heavy vehicles to withstand powerful improvised explosive devices

The German Leopard I main battle tank has been praised as an example of post-war engineering excellence. The Leopard I was widely exported to other countries during the 1980s.

94

An Iraqi T-72 fires its 4.9-in (125-mm) gun during exercises. Produced in greater numbers than any other tank in history, variants of the T-72 continue in service following numerous upgrade programs.

(IEDs) and to function effectively and efficiently in an urban environment where speed and firepower are somewhat nullified by narrow streets and vulnerable civilian populations.

Israeli incursions into Lebanon in the last quarter century, the intervention of the U.S. and British-led Coalition in Iraq, and NATO involvement in Afghanistan have provided graphic evidence of the need to improve tank performance in an urban setting. For example, the Israelis have outfitted their Merkava with urban warfare equipment, and the Americans have fitted many of their Abrams main battle tanks with the TUSK (Tank Urban Survival Kit). Other nations have done the same.

Although close-quarter fighting is as challenging today as it was decades ago, tanks and mechanized infantry continue to excel in open country, where fast-moving mutual support and the combination of survivability, speed, and devastating firepower remain lethal. The battlefield of tomorrow will undoubtedly pose yet unknown challenges; however, the tank is destined to remain a principal instrument of attack and defense.

"They [Iraqi forces] had Soviet equipment, they had French equipment, they had British equipment… they had three different generations of Soviet tank from a very early rudimentary generation of T-55, all the way up to the T-72 which was a very, very good tank."

General Norman Schwarzkopf, commander of Coalition ground forces during the 1991 Gulf War

T-62

The Soviet T-62 was developed during the late 1950s, but it was not revealed to the public until 1965. By that time, its shortcomings were evident. A slight improvement to the T-54/55, it remained inferior to Western designs throughout its career as the front-line Soviet tank.

TURRET
The readily identifiable egg-shaped turret was carried over from the T-54/55. It provided good protection but limited the depression of the main weapon.

MAIN ARMAMENT
The 4.5-in (115-mm) smoothbore U-5TS high-velocity cannon was distinguished from the 3.9-in (100-mm) D-10T cannon of the T-54/55 by its greater length and the addition of a bore evacuator.

ARMOR PROTECTION
At 4 in (102 mm) on the frontal glacis and 3.1 in (79 mm) on the upper sides of the hull, and sloped at 60 degrees, the armor protection of the T-62 was effectively doubled but still considered inadequate. The turret front was protected by a maximum 9.4 in (240 mm) of armor.

- More than 20,000 T-62 tanks were built in the Soviet Union and Czechoslovakia during the 1960s.

- Long after Soviet production ceased, North Korea continued to build a modified T-62.

- Vehicles utilizing the T-62 chassis included the self-propelled SU-130 assault gun, a flamethrower tank, and a recovery vehicle.

COMMANDER POSITION
Seated to the upper left inside the turret, with the loader to his right and the gunner forwards and below, the commander viewed the field through four periscopes, which were integral with his rotating cupola.

ENGINE
The 12-cylinder, 581-hp (433-kW) V-55-5 diesel engine powered the T-62 at a maximum road speed of 30 mph (50 km/h) with a range of 310 miles (500 km) on the road.

DRIVER COMPARTMENT
Seated forwards and to the left in the hull, the driver had a pair of observation periscopes, which could be changed for infrared vision.

SUSPENSION
The modified Christie suspension included five oversize bogies but lacked return rollers. Its traction was good, but it was prone to throwing tracks at high speed.

Marginally inferior to 1960s vintage Western tanks, the T-62 had all the virtues and vices of the T-54/55. It was fairly easy to maintain, had good mobility, a low silhouette, and an excellent gun. On the other hand, the vehicle was a cramped "ergonomic slum."

RIVAL: T-64

T-62 – SPECIFICATION

Country of Origin: Soviet Union
Crew: 4
Designer: OKB-520 design bureau
Designed: late 1950s–1961
Manufacturer: Uralvagonzavod
Produced: 1961–75 (USSR); 1975–78 (Czechoslovakia); until 1980s (North Korea)
Number Built: More than 22,700
In Service: July 1961–present
Weight: 44.09 tons (40 tonnes)

Dimensions:
Length (with barrel): 30.6 ft (9.34 m)
Length (hull): 21.75 ft (6.63 m)
Width: 10.83 ft (3.30 m)
Height: 7.87 ft (2.40 m)

Performance:
Speed, Road: 31 mph (50 km/h)
Speed, Cross-country: 24.9 mph (40 km/h)
Range, On Road: 279.6 miles (450 km) (404 miles [650 km] with two extra 52.8 gallon [200 l] fuel tanks)
Range, Cross-country: 199 miles (320 km) (279.6 miles [450 km] with two extra 52.8 gallon [200 l] fuel tanks)
Suspension: Torsion bar

Engine:
Powerplant: 1 x V-55 12-cylinder 4-stroke one-chamber 10.2 gallon (38.88 l) water-cooled diesel producing 581 hp (433 kW) at 2,000 rpm
Power/weight: 14.5 hp (10.8 kW) per ton
Fuel capacity: 253.6 gallons (960 l)

Armor and Armament:
Armor Type: Cast turret
Turret Front: 9.53 in (242 mm)
Turret Sides: 6.02 in (153 mm)
Turret Rear: 3.82 in (97 mm)
Turret Roof: 1.56 in (40 mm)
Hull Front: 4.02 in (102 mm) at 60 degrees
Hull Upper Sides: 3.11 in (79 mm)
Hull Lower Sides: 0.59 in (15 mm)
Hull Rear: 1.8 in (46 mm) at 0 degrees
Hull Bottom: 0.79 in (20 mm)
Hull Roof: 1.22 in (31 mm)
Main Armament: 1 x 4.5-in (115-mm) U-5TS (2A20) smoothbore gun. 40 rounds
Secondary Armament: 1 x 0.3-in (7.62-mm) PKT coaxial general-purpose machine gun (2500 rounds); 1 x 0.5-in (12.7-mm) DShK 1938/46 anti-aircraft heavy MG (Optional until T-62 Obr. 1972)

Variants:
T-62: Base production vehicle.
T-62K: Commander's vehicle.
T-62D: Additional armor and specialized anti-tank system.
T-62D-1: Updated T-62D variant with newer powerplant.
T-62M: Modifications including anti-tank defense system and added passive armor.
T-62M1: Updated engine; added passive armor.
T-62M1-1: Without passive armor and anti-armor defense system.
T-62MV: Features explosive reactive armor.
T-62 Flamethrower Vehicle: Added flamethrower to turret.

T-62

T-62, T-64 AND TYPE 69

The T-62A (shown), incorporated a 0.5-in (12.7-mm) DshK anti-aircraft machine gun in addition to the coaxial 0.3-in (7.62-mm) machine gun, which was used for close defense against infantry. Although it also included a stabilized main gun, which theoretically allowed for firing on the move, the 4.5-in (115-mm) cannon could not be loaded while the turret was being traversed, minimizing any advantages it brought. The T-62 has been referred to as a stretched version of the T-55 with a larger hull and turret ring. Such changes were necessary to absorb the recoil of the 4.5-in (115-mm) gun. However, a top-loading breech and other factors limited the rate of fire to a maximum of four rounds per minute.

The T-64 was introduced in the 1960s and was a more advanced version of the T-62; a revolutionary feature of the T-64 was the incorporation of an automatic loader for its 4.5-in (115-mm) gun, allowing a crew member's position to be omitted.

Some of the components of the T-62 were copied in the Chinese Type 69; this was after a Soviet T-62 tank was captured by the PLA in 1969.

CHINESE VARIANT: TYPE 69

Painted in mottled camouflage, this T-62 presents an ominous sight with its 4.5-in (115-mm) U5TS smoothbore main cannon. Note the thermal sleeve on the weapon's barrel and the externally mounted fuel tank.

The T-62 remained the standard Soviet main battle tank from the mid-1960s until the late 1970s, when it was superseded by the T-64 and T-72, which was developed rapidly and purchased by the armed forces of numerous non-Warsaw Pact nations.

At the height of the Cold War, it was apparent to Soviet tank designers that their T-54/55 main battle tank could not penetrate the frontal armor of NATO tanks, such as the U.S. Patton or British Centurion with its 3.9-in (100-mm) main weapon firing armor-piercing shells. When an attempt to upgun the T-55 to a 4.5-in (115-mm) main gun failed, a larger hull and turret ring were engineered to mount the heavier U-5TS cannon. In this way, the T-62 was born.

While the T-62 did provide improvements over the T-54/55, such as better armament, reinforced hull bottom armor to protect against mines, a thermal sleeve for the main gun, and rubber track pads, the tank remained quite similar to its predecessor. The interior was laid out in typical Soviet style, with little consideration for the comfort of the four-man crew. While the T-62 maintained the qualities of low silhouette, good cross-country mobility, and ease of maintenance, its functionality in combat continued to suffer.

FIRING FAILINGS

The entire firing procedure was cumbersome at best. The commander acquired the target through a stadiametric sight, then rotated the turret to the proper position. At that point, the gunner took over, sighting the weapon and then firing. After firing, the gun would go into détente for the spent cartridge to eject, and traversing the turret was not possible while loading. An open driver's hatch prevented the turret from traversing as well, and the low turret ceiling was even more restrictive, particularly when attempting to fire on targets at lower grade than the T-62.

Further, the gunner was required to heave a 50-lb (23-kg) ammunition round into the breech left-handed. The main gun had been stabilized, but the outdated fire controls virtually eliminated this improvement. The low rate of fire resulted in few second-chance successes, and the poor fire control limited the effective range of the 4.5-in (115-mm) gun from its 6560-ft (2000-m) limit to about half that distance.

The turret of the T-62 was lined with leaded foam to protect against radiation, and an NBC (nuclear, biological, chemical) defense filtration system was incorporated. Although such movement was hazardous, the tank was capable of deploying a snorkel and traversing water up to 13 ft (4 m) deep. However, the tank's armor protection was considered inadequate and ammunition storage in the hull near the tank's fuel supply could produce devastating results if the armor was penetrated. The advantage of its low maintenance was tempered by the fact that the components of the T-62, particularly the 581-hp (433-kW), 12-cylinder V-55-5 diesel engine, transmission, and tracks, were of inferior quality and only half as durable as those of contemporary Western tanks.

The T-62 saw combat during the Iran-Iraq War of the 1980s, the Middle East conflicts, the Soviet invasion of Afghanistan, and in Angola. Antiquated Iraqi T-62s were also destroyed in large numbers during the first Gulf War as a new generation of main battle tanks eclipsed any improvements to the original version. Modernized variants continue to serve with the armies of such nations as Egypt, Iran, Cuba, Libya, Syria, and Vietnam.

Interior view

The turret of the Soviet T-62 heavy tank was cramped and allowed little room for crewmen to reposition themselves. Its low ceiling also restricted the depression of the main armament.

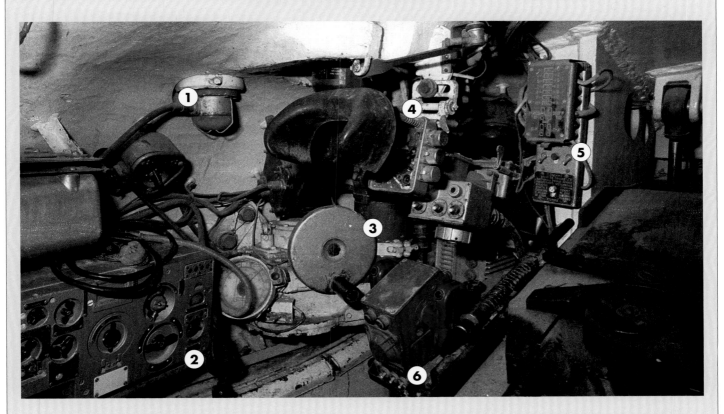

(1) **Interior Lighting:** A small light mounted on the interior of the T-62 turret provided some illumination during operations.

(2) **Electrical Circuitry:** The T-62 depended on electrical current to operate multiple systems within the tank, and circuitry was in several positions throughout the hull and turret.

(3) **Manual Travers Crank:** In the event of a power failure or battle damage, the turret could be traversed manually using this combination of wheel and handle.

(4) **Elevation Equipment:** The angle of elevation of the main cannon was controlled from the gunner's position with powered switches.

(5) **Communication Equipment:** The gunner was provided with his own junction box, which was attached to the hull on his left side next to the AM 1780/VRC radio mount.

(6) **Gunner's Controls:** The gunner controlled the sighting and firing of the main cannon with stabilization, elevation, and traverse controls and a main and back-up trigger system.

M113

Conceived as a battle taxi to deliver infantry to combat zones and then withdraw, the M113 armored personnel carrier evolved into a fighting vehicle. Its chassis has served as the platform for numerous special-purpose vehicles since the 1960s.

TROOP ACCESS
Combat troops entered and exited the standard vehicle by means of a powered ramp door or through a large rectangular roof hatch.

HULL CONSTRUCTION
The box-like hull of the M113 is watertight, welded aluminium armor, and its forward edges slope at 60 degrees.

MAIN ARMAMENT
The M106 mortar carrier variant with ACAV modifications (shown) mounts a 4.2-in (107-mm) mortar. This can be fired from inside the troop compartment on a turntable platform or set up outside the vehicle. Its 0.5-in (12.7-mm) machine gun is protected against small-arms fire by shields.

FACTS

- The M113 armored personnel carrier entered service in 1960 and was deployed to Vietnam.
- The M113 chassis serves as the basis for gun carriers, recovery vehicles, and missile systems.
- More than 4500 M113s have been produced under license by the Italian manufacturer OTO Melara.

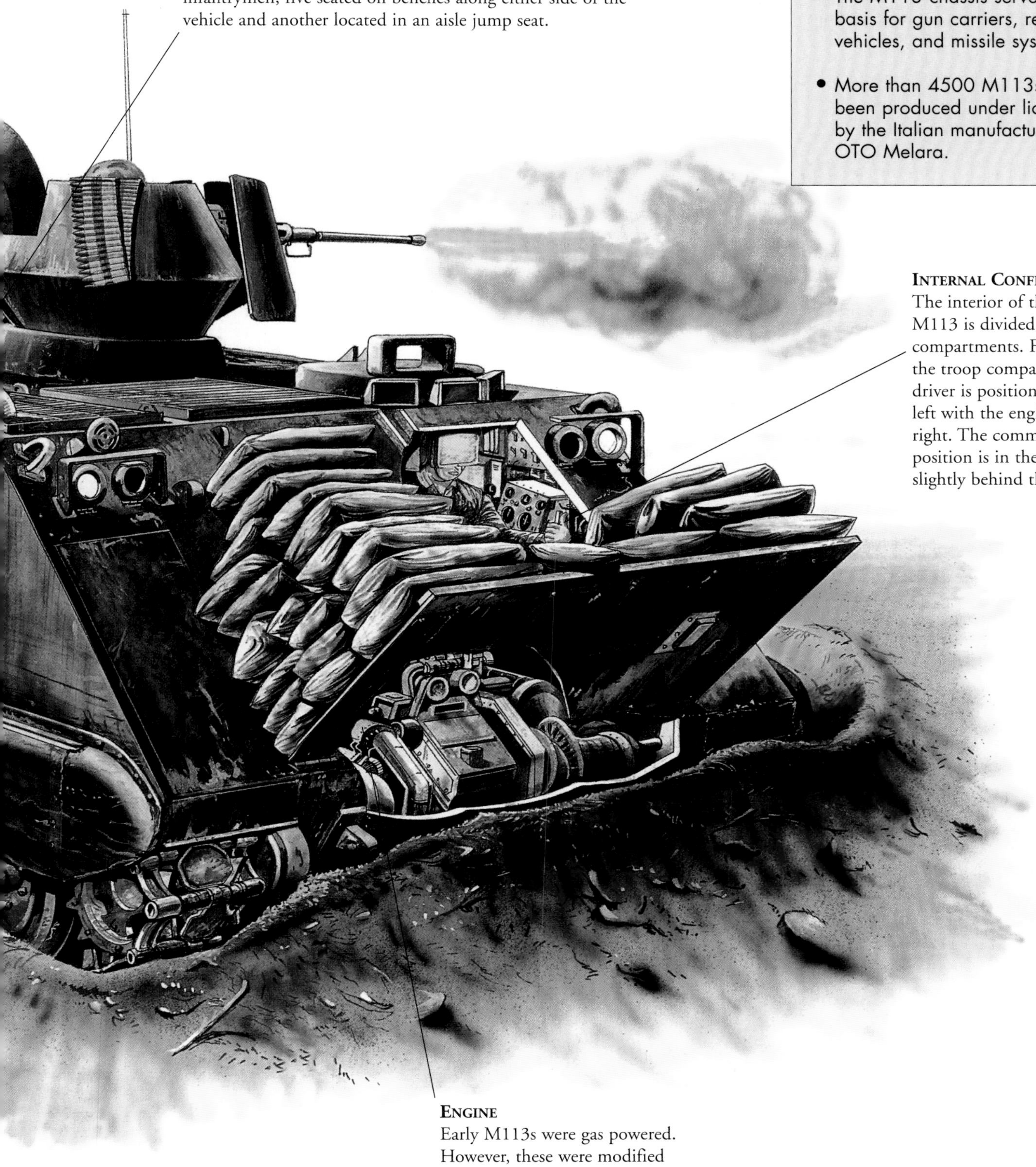

TROOP CAPACITY
The interior of the standard M113 armored personnel carrier is capable of transporting up to 11 combat-ready infantrymen, five seated on benches along either side of the vehicle and another located in an aisle jump seat.

INTERNAL CONFIGURATION
The interior of the standard M113 is divided into two compartments. Forward of the troop compartment, the driver is positioned to the left with the engine on his right. The commander's position is in the center, slightly behind the driver.

ENGINE
Early M113s were gas powered. However, these were modified beginning with the M113A1 in favor of a 275-hp (205-kW) Detroit Diesel 6V53T powerplant.

The M113 armored personnel carrier proved to be a remarkable vehicle both in the versatility of its applications and in the reliability of its design and construction. The M113 family of vehicles has been applied to nearly every major functional combat area of the U.S. Army.

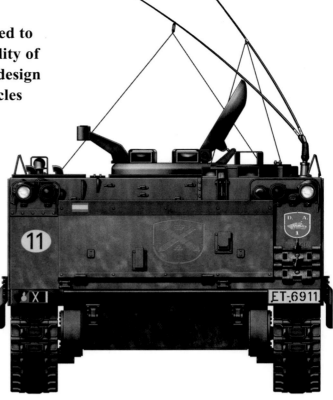

M113 – SPECIFICATION

Country of Origin: USA
Crew: 2 plus 11
Designer: Army Ordnance Tank-Automotive Command (ATAC)
Designed: 1956–60
Manufacturer: Army Ordnance Tank-Automotive Command (ATAC)
In Production: 1960–present
In Service: 1962–present
Numbers Built: 80,000
Weight: 12.43 tons (11.3 tonnes)

Dimensions:
Length: 8 ft 3 in (2.52 m)
Width: 8 ft 10 in (2.69 m)
Height: 6 ft 1 in (1.85 m)

Performance:
Speed, Road: 38 mph (61 km/h)
Speed, Amphibious: 3 mph (5 km/h)
Operational Range: 298 miles (480 km)

Engine:
Powerplant: 1 x General Motors 6V53 6-cylinder diesel, 275 hp (205 kW)
Power/Weight Ratio: 22.36 hp/ton
Suspension: Torsion bar, 5 road wheels

Armor and Armament:
Armor: 1.77 in (45 mm)
Main Armament: Various but minimum usually 1 x 0.5-in (12.7-mm) machine gun

Variants:
M113A1: Starting in 1964, the gas engine was replaced with a diesel engine to take advantage of the better fuel economy and reduced fire hazard of the diesel engine. The suffix A1 was used on all variants to denote a diesel engine.
M113A2: 1979 upgrades including cooling and suspension improvements and smoke grenade launchers on the glacis plate. The suffix A2 is used on all variants to denote upgrade to A2 standard.
M113A3: 1987 further improvements included a yoke for steering instead of laterals, a more powerful engine, external fuel tanks, and internal spall liners for improved protection.
M113 Armored Cavalry Assault Vehicle (ACAV): The Armored Cavalry Assault Vehicle (ACAV) was introduced in the Vietnam War after it was found that the commander and cargo hatch positions were extremely exposed and the vehicle's armament was in many ways inadequate. The kit included shields and circular turret armor for the commander's Browning M-2 0.5-in (12.7-mm) machine gun, and two additional 0.3-in (7.62-mm) M60 machine guns, again with shields, fitted on either side of the top cargo hatch.

VARIANT: M113 FITTER

M113

The M113 was not designed as an armored fighting vehicle, but the exigencies of combat, particularly in Vietnam, caused its role to rapidly evolve and brought about a number of fighting versions. The M106 variant mounts a 4.2-in (107-mm) mortar on a turntable and is distinguished by its three-piece circular hatch above the modified troop compartment rather than the standard single hatch. The mortar may be removed from the vehicle for combat or fired from inside with the large ramp to the rear closed. Other mortar variants of the M113 include the M125, armed with a 3-in (81-mm) mortar, and the M121 with a 4.7-in (120-mm) weapon. A huge range of M113 variants exist, ranging from infantry carriers to nuclear missile carriers.

VARIANT: M113A1 DOZER

The role of the M113 armored personnel carrier extended beyond that of a battle taxi for delivering personnel during the Vietnam War. The M113 became a fighting vehicle, and numerous variants were produced in response to the particular requirements of combat.

Designed to be smaller, less expensive, lighter, and faster than its predecessor, the M59, the M113 may well be the most highly modified armored vehicle in history, ranging from troop carrier to fighting vehicle and weapons platform. Its versatility has lengthened its service life substantially.

An icon of U.S. involvement in Vietnam, the M113 armored personnel carrier was developed as a vehicle to deliver infantry into combat. However, the role of the M113 continued to evolve during the next half-century.

Following a series of trials that had begun in the mid-1950s, the M113, developed by Ford Machinery Corporation (FMC), entered service in 1960 as a lighter, faster APC with amphibious capabilities. It could be deployed by air, and had a suitable capacity for troop transport.

CONSPICUOUS BUT SWIFT

The box-like M113 hull design is built of watertight, welded aluminium armor, considered superior to a similar hull of steel construction, with the glacis sloped at 60 degrees as added protection against anti-tank explosive charges. Early M113s were powered by the 215-hp (160-kW) Chrysler V-8 75M gas engine. With a height of 8 ft 2 in (2.5 m), the silhouette of the

M113 is somewhat conspicuous. However, its ground speed exceeds 40 mph (64 km/h). Its armor protection, ranging from 0.4–1.5 in (12–38 mm), is adequate against small arms and shell fragments. Amphibious track action allows the M113 to travel through water at speeds of nearly 3.5 mph (6 km/h).

The interior of the M113 is divided into two main compartments, with space for 11 combat soldiers seated to the rear. The driver sits forward and to the left with the engine on his right, and the commander sits behind the engine. The commander's cupola has five observation periscopes, while the driver has four, plus an interchangeable infrared night scope. Standard armament includes a single 0.5-in (12.7-mm) M2 machine gun, although a myriad of variants have mounted numerous weapons systems.

In the autumn of 1962, the U.S. Army accepted the M113A1, but replaced the Chrysler engine with the 275-hp (205-kW) General Motors Detroit Diesel 6V53T engine. This reduced the risk of fire substantially and extended the vehicle's range to approximately 300 miles (480 km). In 1979, the M113A2, with a more efficient method of air-cooling the engine, externally mounted fuel tanks, and improvements to the torsion bar suspension, was introduced. By 1987, combat experience had resulted in another principal variant with the M113A3. Bolt holes for the installation of more armor plate were added, as was the RISE

(Reliability Improvements for Selected Equipment) package, including the fuel-efficient Allison X200-4 hydraulic transmission, improved steering and power brakes, and a turbocharged engine. Many of the M113A2 vehicles were also upgraded with the RISE package.

The M113 earned its reputation as an efficient combat vehicle during the Vietnam War. Several upgrades included the addition of machine guns, firing ports for infantry from inside the vehicle, and armor shields to protect the roof machine gunner. Further variants to the M113 chassis have mounted mortars, anti-aircraft guns, and missile systems. The most famous modification was the Vietnam-era ACAV (Armored Cavalry Assault Vehicle). Along with shields for the exposed 0.5-in (12.7-mm) position, the ACAV had a pair of side-mounted shielded 0.3-in (7.62-mm) machine guns. These ACAV kits were manufactured by FMC and the Rock Island Arsenal.

Approximately 80,000 M113 variants have been manufactured and have served with the armed forces of at least 50 nations. Still in use today, the vehicle is expected to remain in service for a number of years to come.

Interior view

The spacious interior of the M113 armored personnel carrier could transport up to 11 combat personnel, while the driver, one of three crew members, was seated forwards and to the left.

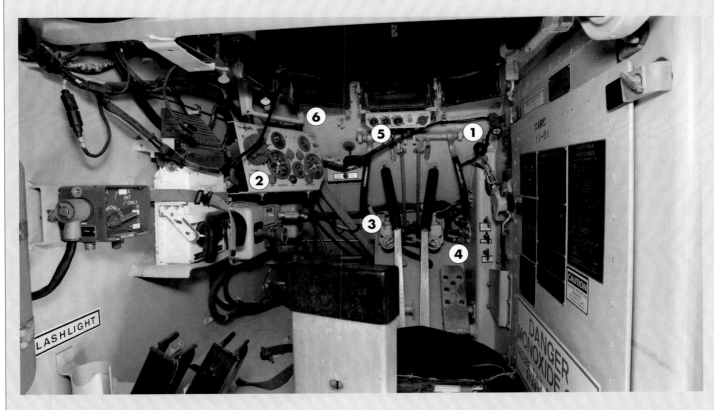

1. **Transmission Shift Lever:** This was set high and to the right of the driver's seat, within easy reach while the vehicle was in motion.

2. **Engine Gauges:** The standard gauges measuring speed, oil pressure, temperature, and other vital signs were positioned high and to the left of the M113 driver.

3. **Steering Levers:** The driver operated the M113 with a pair of steering levers and the transmission shift.

4. **Accelerator Pedal:** The driver operated the accelerator with his right foot, with the ramp-actuating lever to his right.

5. **Warning Light Panel:** From the left, the warning lights indicated high temperatures for differential oil, transmission oil, and engine oil.

6. **Driver Periscopes:** Three of the nine periscopes used by the driver to survey the surrounding terrain are visible here.

Chieftain Mark 5

Although its conceptualization began in the 1940s as a replacement for the Centurion series and a counter to a new generation of Soviet tanks, the Chieftain main battle tank embodied a departure from traditional British design. It did not enter service until the mid-1960s.

FIRE CONTROL
Early Chieftain Marks utilized a 0.5-in (12.7-mm) machine gun mounted above the L11A5 cannon to assist in target acquisition for the main armament. This was replaced with a laser rangefinder in later variants.

MAIN ARMAMENT
The 4.7-in (120-mm) L11A5 cannon was, for its time, the most powerful weapon mounted on a tank in the world.

ARMOR PROTECTION
The frontal glacis of the Chieftain was 8 in (203 mm) thick and it sloped at 70 degrees, which essentially doubled its thickness. The thickness of the side armor is estimated at 1.5 in (38 mm) and turret armor at 7.6 in (195 mm).

HULL DESIGN
Composed of several steel sections welded together, the Chieftain hull followed standard British design, with a driver compartment to the front, fighting compartment in the center, and engine compartment to the rear.

F A C T S

- At more than 60 tons (54 tonnes), the weight of the Chieftain proved a handicap to maneuvering cross-country.

- The first Chieftain prototype was delivered by Leyland in 1961.

- An Iranian order for 1400 Shir II variants was cancelled after the fall of the Shah's government.

TURRET
Cast in two pieces, which were then welded together, the turret had a distinctively pronounced slope, and housed the commander, gunner, and loader.

ENGINE
The 750-hp (559-kW) Leyland L60 No. 4 Mk 8A 12-cylinder multi-fuel engine – capable of using diesel or gas – powered the Chieftain Mark 5, while an export version was equipped with the 900-hp (671-kW) Rolls-Royce Condor engine.

SUSPENSION
The Horstmann bogey suspension included six road wheels and was protected against explosive blasts by large armor plates.

The Chieftain main battle tank is derived from a long line of tanks that began with the Matilda in 1939. The Matilda's successors evolved from infantry support through cruiser to main battle tank as they were made progressively faster and upgunned.

CHIEFTAIN MARK 5

CHIEFTAIN MARK 5 – SPECIFICATION

Country of Origin: United Kingdom
Crew: 4
Designer: Leyland Motors
Designed: 1956
Manufacturer: Leyland Motors
In Production: 1963–early 1970s
In Service: 1963–96
Number Built: 900
Gross Weight: 60.5 tons (55 tonnes)

Dimensions:
Hull Length: 24.7 ft (7.52 m)
Length (Gun forward): 35.4 ft (10.8 m)
Width: 11.5 ft (3.5 m) (over skirts)
Overall Height: 9.5 ft (2.9 m)

Performance:
Maximum Speed: 30 mph (50 km/h)
Range, Road: 310 miles (500 km)
Range, Cross-country: Approx. 180 miles (300 km)
Ground Pressure: 0.9 kg/cm^2
Fording Capacity: 3.5 ft (1.07 m) (15 ft [4.6 m] with preparation)
Maximum Gradient: 37 degrees
Maximum Trench Width: 10.3 ft (3.15 m)
Maximum Vertical Obstacle: 3 ft (0.9 m)
Suspension Type: Horstmann

Engine:
Powerplant: 1 x Leyland L60 No.4 Mark 8A vertically opposed 12 cyl. liquid-cooled compression-ignition 2-stroke multifuel
Capacity: n/a
Output: 750 bhp/560 kW @ 2100 rpm
Power/Weight Ratio: 13.6 bhp/ton
Fuel Capacity: 210 gallons (955 l)

Armament and Armor:
Main Armament: 1 x 4.7-in (120-mm) L11A5 L/56
Secondary Armament: 1 x 0.5-in (12.7-mm) L21 ranging MG; 1 x 0.3-in (7.62-mm) L8 GP MG
Ancillary Armament: 1 x 0.3-in (7.62-mm) L37 GP MG in AA mount
Armor Type: Homogeneous cast/welded nickel-steel with cast/welded turret plus Stillbrew composite steel/ceramic appliqué panels

Variants:
Mark 2: Fitted with 650 bhp (484 kW) engine.
Mark 3: Improved Chieftain.
Mark 5: Featured an uprated engine.
Mark 5/2K: Kuwaiti export models; 165 examples delivered.
Mark 6: Standardization of previous production Mark; ranging machine gun added to main gun.
Mark 7: Revised engine.
Mark 8: Resilient mantlet and new commander's cupola.
Mark 9: Revised intermediate production Mark; IFCS (Improved Fire Control System).
Mark 10: Revised intermediate production Mark; IFCS; night and all-weather fighting capability with Thermal Observation and Gunnery Sight implementation.
Mark 11: Revised intermediate production Mark; IFCS; "Stillbrew" passive armor.
"Shir 1": Modified for Iranian export; later named "Khalid."
"Shir 2": Iranian export; 1225 examples ordered but never produced or delivered due to the regime change in 1979.
ARV: Armored Recovery Vehicle.
AVLB: Armored Bridgelayer.
AVRE: Armored Vehicle Royal Engineers.
Chieftain ARRV: Armored Recovery and Repair Vehicle.

VARIANT: CHIEFTAIN 900

CHIEFTAIN MK 5

The interior of the Chieftain, as shown in the Mark 5, which was the final production variant, included a semi-reclining position for the driver. Such a configuration facilitated the tank's low silhouette, while sloping armor contributed to a less conspicuous profile and effectively doubled the protection afforded the crew of four. The commander, gunner, and loader were stationed in the low, sleek turret, which did not include a gun mantlet and allowed greater concealment in the hull-down position. The Mark 5 included improvements to the engine and the introduction of a nuclear, biological, and chemical (NBC) defense system.

VARIANT: CHIEFTAIN AVRE

The Chieftain main battle tank is distinguishable by its sloping turret and the imposing 4.7-in (120-mm) L11A5 cannon it mounts. Deployed at the height of the Cold War, the Chieftain was Britain's response to the heavy Soviet tanks of the era.

In the 1960s, the Chieftain main battle tank was, for a time, the most powerful fighting vehicle of its kind in the world. Its 4.7-in (120-mm) L11A5 main cannon was the heaviest weapon then deployed in a tank.

By the time the Chieftain was deployed with the British army in the 1960s, the Cold War was at its height. By then, the need for a main battle tank that combined maximum firepower with mobility and well protected armor was considered paramount. The Soviet T-54/55 series was well known to military intelligence, and the lessons learned during World War II still resonated among armor engineers.

Conceived as a replacement for the aging Centurion series, the specifications for the new Chieftain were drawn in 1958. By 1961, Leyland Motors produced the first prototypes. The first operational Chieftain entered service with the British army two years later. Immediately, the Chieftain was recognized as the most powerfully armed tank then fielded. It remained so until the introduction of the German Leopard series some time later. The 4.7-in (120-mm) L11A5 main gun of the Chieftain was notable for its power to

penetrate armor and for the fact that it fired charges and projectiles that were separate rather than encased in combination. This was a major survivability improvement, reducing the potential for a catastrophic explosion.

The main gun was initially laid with the assistance of a 0.5-in (12.7-mm) ranging machine gun that fired tracers to mark targets. However, this was replaced in later variants with a laser rangefinder. Secondary armament included a coaxial 0.3-in (7.62-mm) machine gun and a second machine gun of the same size situated on top of the turret near the commander's cupola.

Early Chieftains were powered by a 585-hp (436-kW) diesel engine, but this proved inadequate and was updated in 1967 with the 750-hp (560-kW) Leyland L60 No. 4 Mark 8, while an export version utilized the 900-hp (671-kW) Rolls-Royce Condor. Although an upgrade, the L60 was still considered less than adequate to move the 60-ton (54-tonne) vehicle at a reasonable speed, particularly across country. Its reliability was found to be dubious as well, with a breakdown rate approaching 90 percent. The Horstmann suspension featured six road wheels and heavy armor side plates for added protection against projectiles and to reduce the possibility of the tracks being disabled.

MOBILITY VERSUS POWER

The interior of the Chieftain followed the standard British layout, with the driver forward, the fighting compartment and the centered turret behind, and the engine compartment in the rear. The driver sat in a semi-reclined position and steered the tank with conventional hydraulic tillers and external disc brakes. The commander sat in the turret to the right beneath the rotating cupola and viewed the field through 360-degree periscopes, while the gunner was below and to his front with the loader on the left, both also in the turret. Infrared sights were available to the commander and the gunner, while an externally mounted infrared searchlight was attached on the left side of the turret.

The Chieftain's mobility was restricted by its standard powerplant and unremarkable top speed of 30 mph (48 km/h) on the road. The final production model was the Mark 5, and upgrades continued until a total of 12 variants were offered with further enhancements of engine performance, optics, or improved systems. The Middle East was a lucrative market for export versions of the Chieftain, such as the Shir I and II. The armies of Iran, Kuwait, Jordan, and Oman are among the countries that have purchased it.

Interior view

The Chieftain Mark 5 main battle tank was a mainstay of British forces in Europe during the Cold War. Its interior was in keeping with previous British designs, but it had significant turret modifications.

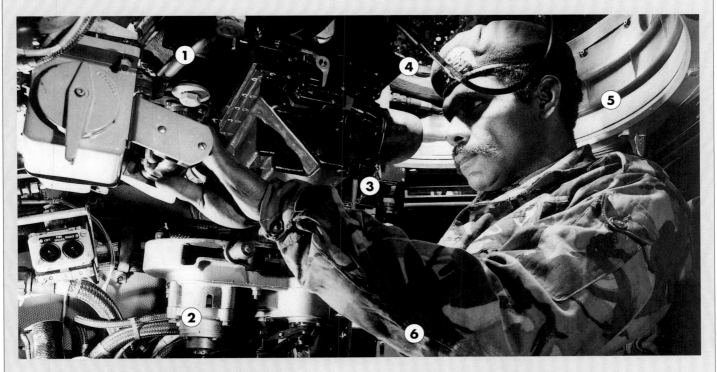

(1) **Laser Rangefinding Equipment:** This increases the accuracy of the main 4.7-in (120-mm) L11A5 cannon.

(2) **Electronic Equipment:** Numerous systems converge inside the turret, including equipment for target acquisition, gun laying, various defenses, and communications.

(3) **Optics:** Image-intensifying day and night vision equipment are used by the crew of the Chieftain Mark 5.

(4) **Sloped Turret:** This allowed freer movement within the confining area, improved armor protection, and even offered storage space.

(5) **Hatch Opening:** Hatches for the commander and other personnel were located on top of the sloped turret, while the driver assumed a semi-recumbent position in the hull.

(6) **Gunner Position:** The gunner sat in front of the tank commander, while the loader sat to his left.

Leopard 1

The first main battle tank developed in post-war West Germany, the Leopard 1 began as a joint venture with France. However, when the combined effort failed, the Germans pursued their own design independently. By 1965, the Leopard 1 was placed in service.

TURRET
The elongated cast turret of the Leopard 1 was modified several times and included an ammunition resupply hatch to the left, a searchlight attached above the 4.1-in (105-mm) gun, and a storage area to the rear.

MAIN ARMAMENT
A German-built version of the proven 4.1-in (105-mm) British Royal Ordnance L7A3 L/52 rifled cannon served as the primary weapon of the Leopard 1 and many other Western main battle tanks.

ARMOR PROTECTION
The sloped frontal hull armor of the Leopard was 2.76 in (70 mm) thick, while the turret mantlet was protected with 2.3 in (60 mm) and less-exposed areas with 0.39–2 in (10–52 mm). The Leopard 1A1 variant added armor side skirts to protect the tracks and wheels.

FACTS

- The West German army issued requirements for a new main battle tank in 1956.
- Although production officially ceased in 1979, the Leopard 1 assembly line was reopened in 1981 to produce tanks for Greece.
- The Italian firm OTO-Melara manufactured the Leopard 1 under license.

SECONDARY ARMAMENT
The Leopard 1 secondary armament consisted of one 0.3-in (7.62-mm) Rheinmetall MG3 machine gun mounted coaxially and a second weapon of the same size pintle-mounted on the commander's hatch.

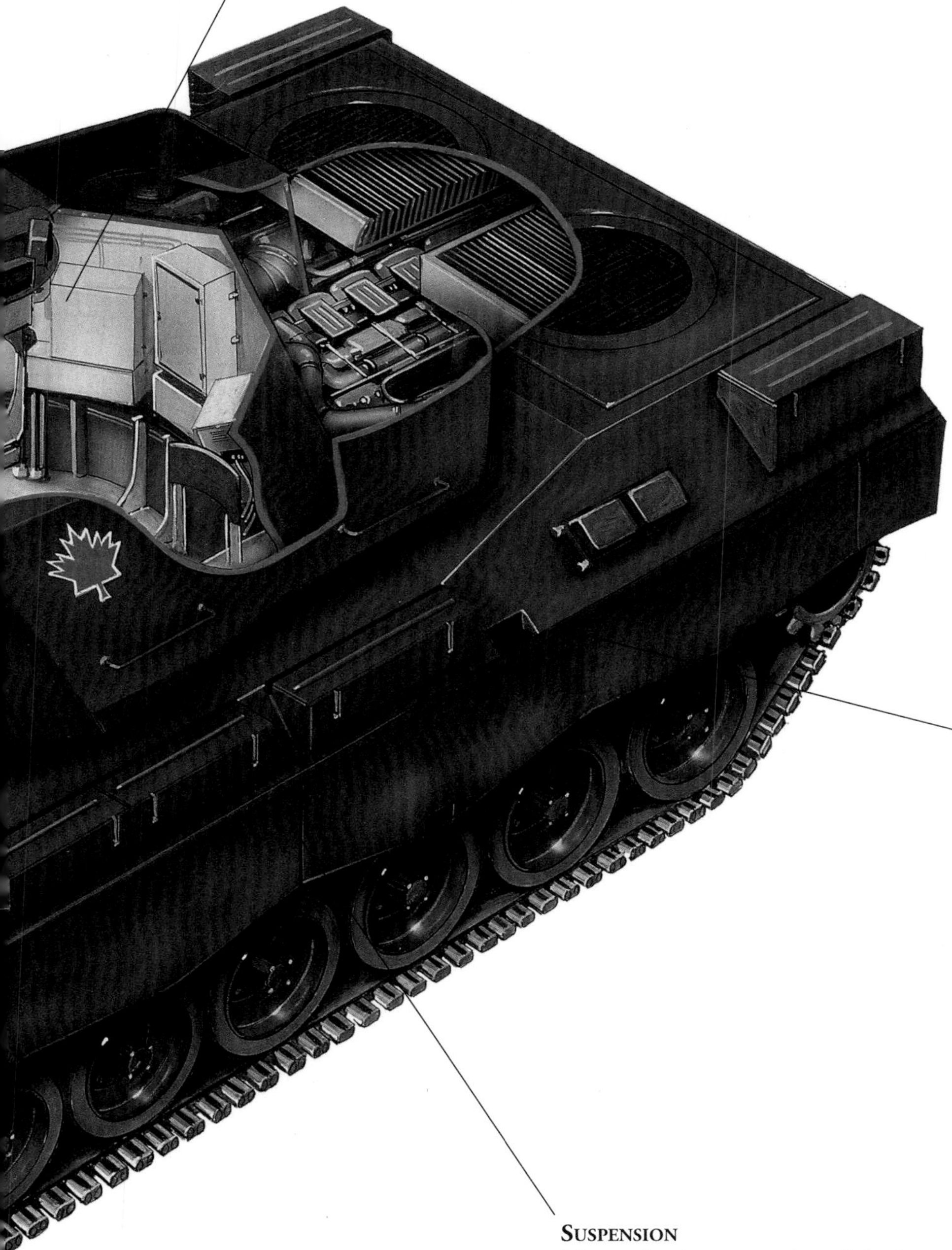

ENGINE
The 830-hp (619-kW), 10-cylinder MTU MB 838 CaM 500 multi-fuel engine was primarily powered by diesel and capable of a top road speed of 40 mph (65 km/h).

SUSPENSION
The torsion bar suspension of the Leopard 1 contributed to the tank's excellent handling during cross-country maneuvers, while its relative light weight at 43 tons (39 tonnes) enhanced its speed and mobility.

At the time that the Leopard 1 was developed, the emphasis of German armored warfare doctrine was on mobility and relatively limited armor protection. The glacis plate, however, was sloped at 60 degrees from the vertical, effectively doubling armor protection.

LEOPARD 1 – SPECIFICATION

Country of origin: West Germany
Crew: 4
Designer: Krauss-Maffei
Designed: Early 1960s
Manufacturers: Oto Melara, Italy
In Production: 1965–79
In Service: 1965–present
Number Built: 5816
Weight: 44 tons (39 tonnes), 46.5 tons (42.2 tonnes) on later models

Dimensions:
Length (gun forward): 31.3 ft (9.54 m)
Length (hull): 27.2 ft (8.29 m)
Width: 11.06 ft (3.37 m)
Height (turret roof): 7.84 ft (2.39 m)
Height (absolute): 8.86 ft (2.7 m)

Performance:
Speed: 40 mph (65 km/h)
Range, Road: 373 miles (600 km)
Range, Cross-country: 280 miles (450 km)

Engine:
Powerplant: 1 x MTU MB 838 Ca M500 10-cylinder, 9.9 gallon (37.4 l) multi-fuel engine generating 830 hp (619 kW) at 2200 rpm
Power/weight: 19.6 PS/ton
Suspension: Torsion bar

Armor and Armament:
Armor: RHA, 0.39–2.76 in (10–70 mm)
Main Armament: 1 x 4.1-in (105-mm) Royal Ordnance L7A3 L/52 rifled gun. 13 rounds in turret, 42 rounds in hull.
Secondary Armament: 2 x 0.3-in (7.62-mm) MG3 or FN MAG (coaxial and commander's hatch). 5500 rounds.

Major Variants:
Leopard 1A1A1: Additional turret armor.
Leopard 1A2: Updated turret function and passive night vision equipment installed.
Leopard 1A3: Improved armor and new all-welded turret production.
Leopard 1A4: Integrated fire control system implemented. This was the last variant used by the German army.
Leopard 1A5: Updated night vision equipment, computerized fire control and became upgraded version for all earlier German army models.
Leopard 1 AVLB: Bridgelayer.
Leopard 1 ARV: Armored Recovery Vehicle.
Leopard 1 AEV: Engineering Vehicle.
Leopard 1 Trainer: Replaced with windowed turret for driver training.
Gepard Flakpanzer: Mobile twin 1.38-in (35-mm) anti-aircraft air defense system (Leopard 1 chassis).

LEOPARD 1

The interior of the Leopard 1 main battle tank was divided into two compartments, with the engine to the rear and separated from the forwards fighting compartment by a firewall. Its crew of four included the driver, positioned in the hull forwards and to the right. The commander and gunner were seated in the cast turret to the right, while the loader was to the left, where he fed shells into the breech of the 4.1-in (105-mm) L7A3 gun by hand. The coaxial 0.3-in (7.62-mm) machine gun was originally utilized for ranging the main weapon. However, this was later upgraded with an optical gunsight.

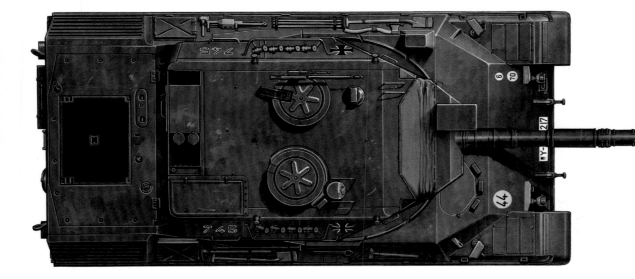

Shown during training exercises, this Leopard 1 main battle tank is painted in winter camouflage. Note the driver's periscope located near the center of the hull and the coaxial FN MAG machine gun mounted near the commander's hatch. This tank was exported to at least 14 countries.

Beginning in 1971, the Federal Republic of Germany initiated a series of modifications to the Leopard 1, including a gun stabilization system enabling the tank to fire on the move. This rectified the Leopard's greatest deficiency, aside from its inadequate armor protection, which was sacrificed for improved mobility.

When the army of the Federal Republic of Germany was reconstituted a decade after the end of World War II, its armored formations were initially equipped with U.S. M48 Patton tanks. Within two years, the government of the German Federal Republic had authorized the development of a new main battle tank, in a joint effort with French designers. The project produced unsatisfactory results, so German engineers pursued their own design, the Leopard 1.

The Leopard 1 prototype was delivered in 1961, and production was initiated by Krauss Maffei of Munich in 1964. The first production Leopard 1 was received by the German army in September 1965. Nearly 6500 main battle tanks and variants were built in Germany and under license by the Italian manufacturer OTO-Melara.

Armed with the German-built L7A3 L/52 4.1-in (105-mm) cannon, originally a British design, the Leopard 1

combined firepower and mobility. The compromise was in protective armor. Even though the armor of both the front glacis and turret were sloped, the protection at a maximum of 2.75 in (70 mm) was considered inadequate. At 43 tons (39 tonnes), the tank was comparatively light, and the 830-hp (619-kW), V-10 multi-fuel engine produced the best power-to-weight ratio of contemporary main battle tanks. It could also be replaced in the field in as little as 20 minutes.

EIGHT PERISCOPES

A crew of four manned the Leopard 1, with the driver viewing the field through three periscopes, one of which could be replaced with infrared equipment for night vision. The gunner and loader were provided with a single scope and stereoscopic rangefinder and a pair of scopes respectively, while the commander could look through any of eight periscopes (one of these capable of infrared replacement) incorporated into his hatch on top of the turret.

The rifled 4.1-in (105-mm) cannon was also deployed with British and U.S. main battle tanks, such as the Centurion and M1 Abrams. The weapon was not stabilized in early production Leopards, but this was corrected with a Cadillac Gage system in the 1A1 variant. The loader was required to place each round of ammunition into the breech by hand, but the spent shell casing was automatically ejected.

Prominent variants of the Leopard 1 included the 1A1. It had a stabilized main gun fitted with a thermal sleeve to reduce warping and maintain accuracy, improved tracks, and armored skirts to protect the tracks and wheels. The 1A1A1, which was upgraded from 1974–77, featured the addition of armor made of reinforced steel plate. This was developed by Blohm and Voss for the turret, gun mantlet, and forward section of the hull. Another notable variant, the 1A1A2, featured a system for intensifying images.

The Leopard 1A2 featured a sturdier cast turret, better night vision equipment, and NBC (nuclear, biological, chemical) defense improvements. The 1A3 introduced a welded turret with a wedge-shaped mantlet and spaced armor. In 1974, the 1A4 was equipped with an upgraded computerized fire control system. Further modifications led to the 1A5 in the early 1980s, and in 1987 the 1A6 introduced a 4.7-in (120-mm) cannon. Other variants included armored engineering, recovery, anti-aircraft, and bridging vehicles.

By the mid-1980s, the Leopard 2 was being introduced, and the German army subsequently relegated the Leopard 1 to reserve units.

Interior view

The turret interior of the German Leopard 1 main battle tank provided space for three crew – commander, gunner, and loader. The commander and gunner cooperated in the acquisition of targets.

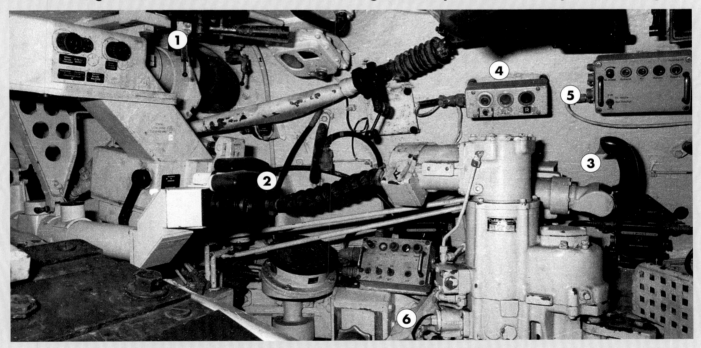

(1) **Gunner's Sights:** The tank's gunner used sophisticated sighting equipment and rangefinding computers to identify targets.

(2) **Gunner's Controls:** At his fingertips, the gunner had controls that traversed the turret and adjusted the elevation of the main weapon to acquire distant targets.

(3) **Commander's Station:** The Leopard 1 commander could also fire the main weapon and used his manual hand station to override the controls when necessary.

(4) **Commander's Control Box:** The commander monitored the systems, several groups of switches, and the gauges.

(5) **Intercom Box:** The commander's intercom box was mounted to the turret hull on the Leopard 1, allowing him to maintain communications with other crew members.

(6) **Gunner's Seat:** This was forwards of the commander's position on the Leopard 1 main battle tank, where he conducted the operation of the 4.1-in (105-mm) cannon.

AAV7

The primary amphibious transport vehicle of the U.S. Marine Corps, the AAV7 is the most recent in a long line of amphibious tracked vehicles designed to insert combat troops and provide fire and logistical support during an inland or cross-country advance.

MAIN ARMAMENT
The AAV7 is equipped with a M242 Bushmaster 0.98-in (25-mm) chain-fed auto-cannon with 900 rounds.

ARMOR PROTECTION
With up to 1.77 in (45 mm) of protective armor, the AAV7 is lighter than its U.S. Army counterpart, the M2/M3 Bradley Fighting Vehicle, but its capacity is much greater.

FACTS

- The AAV7 did not initially include NBC (nuclear, biological, chemical) defense capabilities.
- The Expeditionary Fighting Vehicle (EFV) is slated to replace the AAV7 within the next decade.
- The AAV7 is amphibious without modifications in the field to efficiently cross rivers and streams.

CARGO CAPACITY
The AAV7 is capable of carrying its crew of three along with up to 25 combat-ready marines. In the logistics support role, it is capable of carrying up to 5 tons (4.5 tonnes) of equipment and supplies.

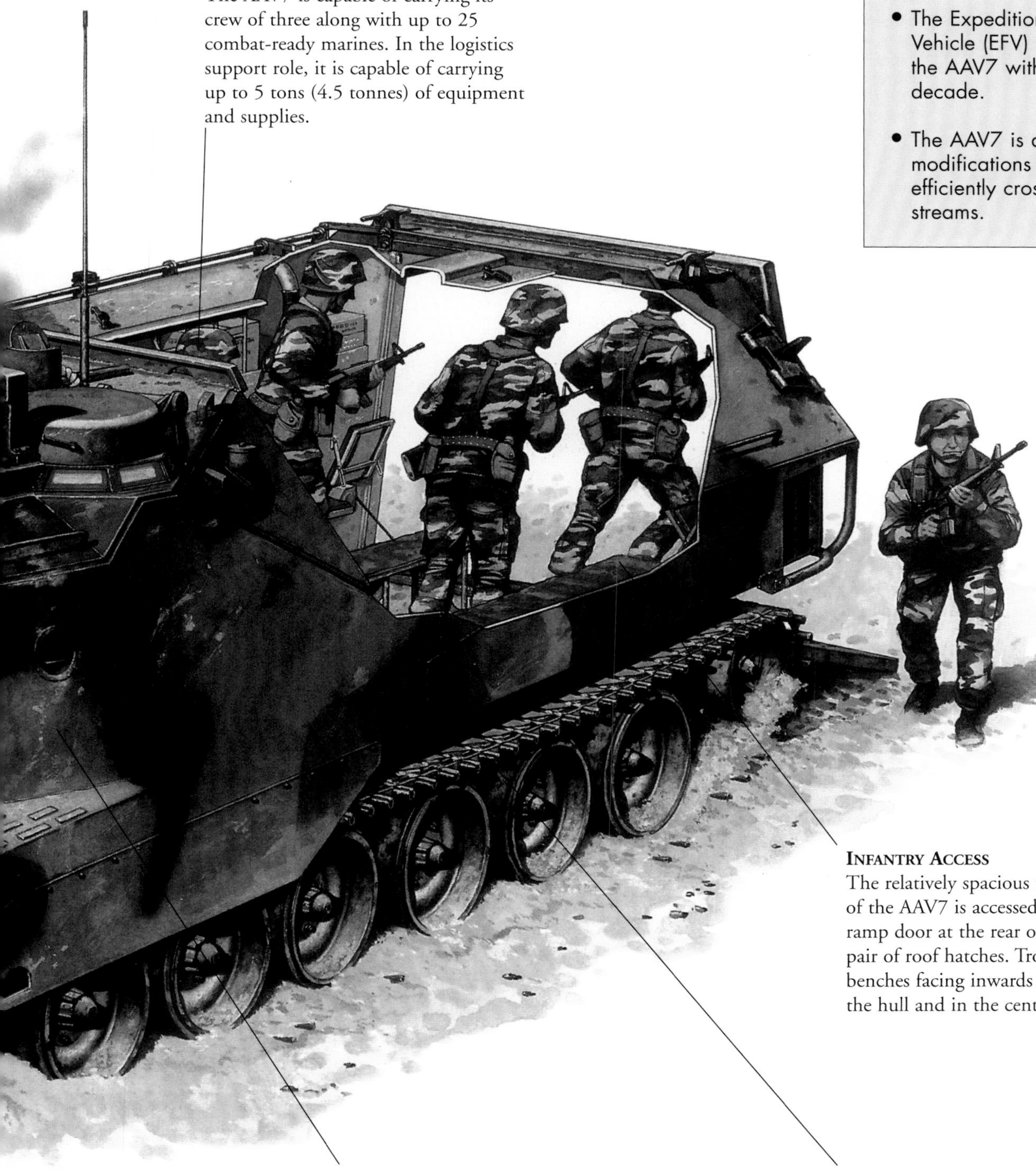

INFANTRY ACCESS
The relatively spacious troop compartment of the AAV7 is accessed through a large ramp door at the rear of the vehicle and a pair of roof hatches. Troops are seated on benches facing inwards along the length of the hull and in the center.

ENGINE
The General Motors Detroit Diesel 8V53T engine was subsequently replaced by the 400-hp (300-kW) Cummins VT 400 903 turbocharged diesel engine, which also has multi-fuel capability.

DRIVE TRAIN
The FMC Corporation HS-400-3A1 transmission drives the tracked vehicle with six rubber-coated road wheels on either side and a torsion bar suspension.

The primary responsibility of the AAV during an amphibious operation is to spearhead a beach assault. It disembarks from a ship and comes ashore, carrying infantry and supplies to provide a forced entry into the amphibious assault area for the surface assault element.

AAV7 – SPECIFICATION

Country of Origin: USA
Crew: 3 + 25
Designer: FMC Corporation
Manufacturer: FMC Corporation
In Production: 1972–
In Service: 1972–present
Number Built: More than 1800
Weight: 25.1 tons (22.8 tonnes)

Dimensions:
Length: 26 ft (7.94 m)
Width: 10.73 ft (3.27 m)
Height: 10.7 ft (3.26 m)

Performance:
Operational Range: 300 miles (480 km)
Speed, Road: 45 mph (64 km/h)
Speed, Cross-country: 8.2 mph (13.5 km/h)

Powerplant:
Engine: 1 x Detroit Diesel 8V-53T (P-7), Cummins VT 400 903 (P-7A1) 400 hp (300 kW); or VTAC 525 903 525 hp (391 kW) (AAV-7RAM-RS)
Power/weight: 18 hp (13 kW) per ton
Suspension: Torsion-bar-in-tube (AAV-7A1); torsion bar (AAV-7RAM-RS)

Armor and Armament:
Armor: 1.77 in (45 mm)
Main Armament: 1 x Mk 19 1.57-in (40-mm) automatic grenade launcher (864 rounds) or M242 Bushmaster 0.98-in (25-mm) (900 rounds)

Secondary Armament: 1 x M2HB 0.5-in (12.7-mm) machine gun (1200 rounds)

Operators:
United States: Marine Corps – 1311.
Argentina: Infanteria de Marina – 21 x LVTP7s.
Brazil: Corpo de Fuzileiros Navais do Brasil – 13 x AAV-7A1, 9 x LVTP-7A1, 2 x LVTC-7A1 and 2 x LVTR-7A.
Cambodia: Royal Cambodian Navy – 63 x AAVT-7s, including 2 x AAVTC-7, 1x AAVTR-7, 9 x AAVTP-7.
Italy: Esercito Italiano – 35 x LVPT7s, 25 of which have been upgraded to AAV-7A1 standard.
South Korea: Republic of Korea Marine Corps – 162.
Republic of China: Republic of China Marine Corps (Taiwan) – 54.
Spain: Spanish Marines (BRIMAR) – 36.
Thailand: Royal Thai Marine Corps – 24.
Venezuela: Venezuelan Navy – 11 x AAVT-7s (1 x AAVTC-7, 1 x AAVTR-7, 9 x AAVTP-7).
Indonesia: Indonesian Marine Corps – 10 units (LVTP7A1) donated by South Korea.
Greece: Hellenic Army – 100 units to be procured from USMC.

AAV7

The AAV7 is divided into two compartments, with the driver forwards and to the left of the transversely mounted engine, the commander and gunner just behind, and the large troop compartment to the rear. The commander is seated below a cupola equipped with seven vision blocks for an all-around view of the surrounding terrain, while the gunner is seated in the turret directly opposite. The driver utilizes seven vision blocks, while an infrared periscope may be fitted for night vision. The 0.5-in (12.7-mm) machine gun is effective in anti-aircraft defense, while the 1.57-in (40-mm) Mark 19 grenade launcher is a lethal anti-personnel weapon.

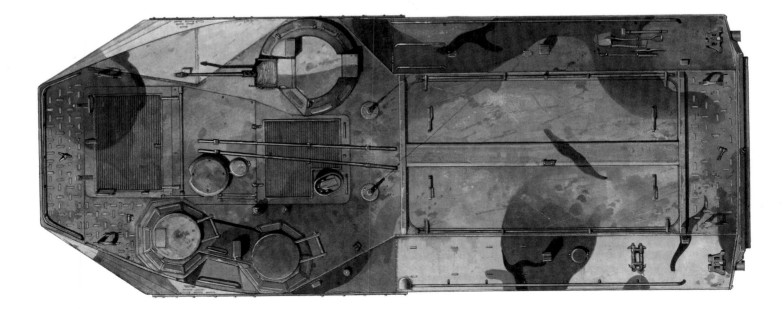

AAVs are deployed during amphibious assaults, during the conduct of river crossings as components of the mechanized task force, and during other special operations ashore. When properly put to use, AAVs are effective in operations after dark, and on a majority of the world's rough terrain.

Amphibious operations in the Pacific theater during World War II demonstrated the need for a tracked amphibious vehicle capable of delivering combat troops ashore, supporting them with direct fire, and transporting supplies and equipment to combat zones. The AAV7 is, therefore, a direct descendant of early landing craft developed to traverse extensive water, coral reefs, sandy beaches, and other terrain.

During the Vietnam War, the U.S. Marine Corps recognized the deficiencies of its relatively short-range LVTP5 series. In 1964, the Corps issued a directive for the development of a replacement vehicle, and the project was undertaken by FMC Corporation, now a division of BAE

Close-up

The AAV7 is the front-line cross-country and urban troop transport vehicle of the U.S. Marine Corps and is capable of carrying up to 25 combat-ready marines.

1. **Cupolas:** Multiple cupolas are on the exterior and at least one of these is often equipped with a 0.5-in (12.7-mm) heavy machine gun.

2. **Sloping Hull:** Configured similarly to the bow of a boat, the forwards hull of the AAV7 contributes to the stability of the amphibious vehicle in water.

3. **Viewing Ports:** Prominent in the silhouette are viewing ports and periscopes, which are available for crew to look through while the vehicle is buttoned up.

4. **Communications Gear:** Antennae for the sending and receiving of data for communications equipment are installed at the rear of the troop compartment.

5. **Entry and Exit:** A large ramp facilitates the rapid entry and exit of up to 25 combat-ready marines from the troop compartment.

6. **Water Jets:** A pair of water jets propel the AAV7 through water at approximately 8 mph (13 km/h).

much broader capabilities. As many as 25 combat-ready marines can be accommodated on three benches – one along the center of the compartment and two on the sides of the hull. Access is gained through a ramp, which folds down, as well as two roof hatches. With the central bench removed and the side benches folded, the cargo capacity of the AAV7 is up to 5 tons (4.5 tonnes).

UPGRADES AND IMPROVEMENTS

An extended service life program was initiated in 1982, upgrading the former LVTP7 to the AAV7A1 configuration. Among the improvements was the installation of a Cummins diesel engine. Electric elevation components for the turret replaced the hydraulics, and an improved torsion bar suspension, smoke grenade launchers, and night vision equipment for the driver were added. In 1987, the Upgunned Weapons Station with the Mk19 1.57-in (40-mm) grenade launcher was added, and along with a 0.5-in (12.7-mm) machine gun, bow planes, magnetic heading systems, and automatic fire suppression capability. By 1992, enhanced appliqué armor had been added. Further upgrades included an improved suspension system and a powerplant similar to the 525-hp (391-kW) engine of the Bradley Fighting Vehicle.

Variants of the AAV7 include the AAVC7A1 command vehicle and the AAVR7A1 recovery vehicle. There is an option to attach mine-clearing equipment as well.

The AAV7 has been deployed in combat with Argentine forces during the 1982 Falklands War and with U.S. forces in Lebanon, Grenada, the Gulf War, and the invasion of Iraq in 2003. The vehicle is currently deployed with the armed forces of at least a dozen countries, and its service life with the U.S. Marine Corps is expected to extend until at least 2015 when its replacement, the Expeditionary Fighting Vehicle (EFV), is scheduled to be available.

Systems' Ground Systems. Two years later, prototypes of a vehicle designated the LVTPX12 were delivered, and by 1971 the first of the new LVTP7 were in service. By 1985, the Marine Corps had changed the vehicle's designation to AAV7 (Amphibious Assault Vehicle).

The AAV7 is constructed of a box-like, watertight welded aluminium hull. It presents a high silhouette, for which the design has been criticized. Shaped like a boat, its bow facilitates movement through water at a speed of 8.2 mph (13.5 km/h), powered by a pair of water jets. On the road and across difficult terrain, its 400-hp (300-kW) Cummins diesel engine powers the AAV7 at speeds of 45 mph (64 km/h).

Although the armor protection is limited at 1.77 in (45 mm) and is known to be substantially less than that of the U.S. Army's Bradley Fighting Vehicle, the AAV7 still has

T-72

Developed primarily for the export market and the satellite states of the Warsaw Pact, the T-72 was produced concurrently with the T-64 main battle tank. In some respects, the T-72 was inferior to its companion, which was intended specifically to equip armored units of the Red Army.

MAIN ARMAMENT
An improved high-velocity 5-in (125-mm) 2A46M cannon, common to the T-64 and the later T-80, fires a variety of shells, including those for piercing armor and high-explosive rounds.

ENGINE
The 780-hp (582-kW), 12-cylinder W-46 diesel engine is also capable of running on benzene and kerosene. Later models were upgraded with a 840-hp (626-kW) engine.

FACTS

- The T-72 is cheaper and easier to produce than its contemporary, the T-64.
- The tank has been built under license in Czechoslovakia, India, the former Yugoslavia, and Poland.
- Six years after production began, the T-72 made its public debut in 1977.

TURRET
Cast from a single piece of steel, the turret of the T-72 retains the characteristic egg shape and is protected to a maximum thickness of 11 in (280 mm) of armor.

CREW COMPARTMENTS
The commander and gunner are seated in the turret to the left and right of the main gun, while the driver's position is forwards and centered in the hull. An automatic loader eliminates the need for a fourth crewman.

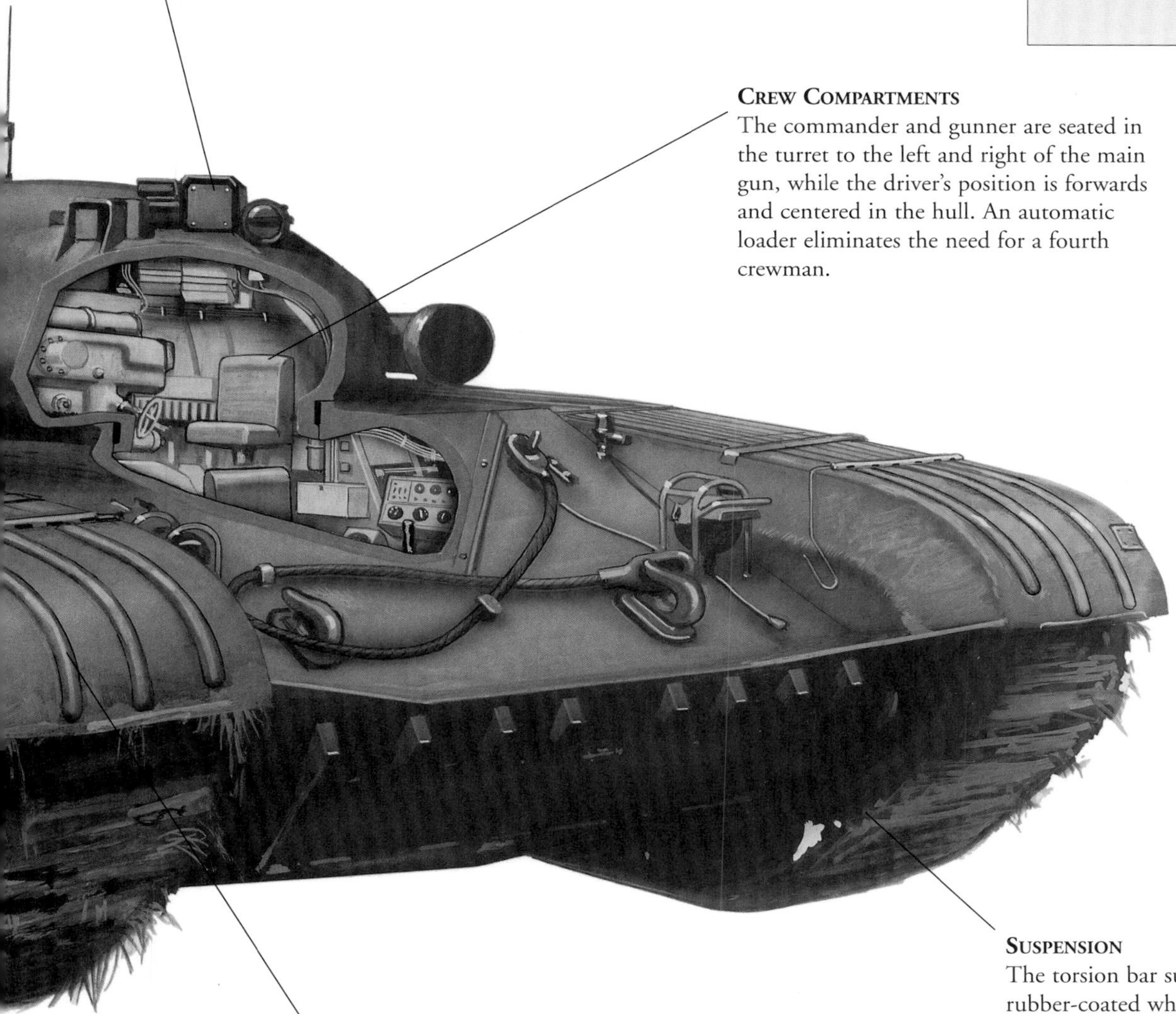

SUSPENSION
The torsion bar suspension supports six cast, rubber-coated wheels with a large drive sprocket, four return rollers, and single-pin tracks with rubber bushed pins. Spring-mounted armor plating protects the upper edges of the wheels.

ARMOR PROTECTION
Consisting of a composite plating of steel, tungsten, ceramic, and plastic, the front glacis of the T-72 is protected with up to 7.8 in (200 mm) of armor. Steel side plates on early models varied in thickness from 1.96–3.1 in (50–80 mm).

Introduced in the early 1970s, the T-72 is not actually a further development of the T-64. Instead, it was a parallel design chosen as a high-production tank complementing the T-64. While the T-64 was deployed only in forwards Soviet units, the T-72 was deployed within the Soviet Union and exported.

T-72A – SPECIFICATION

Country of Origin: Soviet Union
Crew: 3
Designer: Kartsev-Venediktov
Designed: 1967–73
Manufacturer: Uralvagonzavod
Produced: 1971–present
In Service: 1973–present
Number Built: 25,000+
Weight: 45.7 tons (41.5 tonnes)

Dimensions:
Length (gun forward): 31 ft 3 in (9.53 m)
Length (hull): 22 ft 10 in (6.95 m)
Width: 11 ft 9 in (3.59 m)
Height: 7 ft 4 in (2.23 m)

Performance:
Speed: 37 mph (60 km/h)
Operational Range: 290 miles (460 km); 430 miles (700 km) with fuel drums

Powerplant:
Engine: 1 x V-12 diesel 780 hp (582 kW)
Power/weight: 18.8 hp (14.1 kW) per ton
Suspension: Torsion bar
Ground clearance: 19 in (0.49 m)
Fuel capacity: 320 gallons (1200 l)

Armor and Armament:
Armor: 20 in (500 mm) of third-generation composite armor consisting of high-hardness steel, tungsten, and plastic filler with ceramic component
Primary Armament: 1 x 4.9-in (125-mm) 2A46M gun

Secondary Armament: 1 x 0.3-in (7.62-mm) PKT coaxial machine gun, 1 x 0.5-in (12.7-mm) NSVT anti-aircraft machine gun

Variants:
T-72 Ural (1973): Original version.
T-72A (1979): Added laser rangefinder and electronic fire control, turret front and top being heavily reinforced with composite armor (nicknamed "Dolly Parton" by U.S. intelligence), provisions for mounting reactive armor, smoke grenade launchers, flipper armor mount on front mudguards, internal changes.
T-72M: Export "Monkey model" version, similar to T-72A but with thinner armor and downgraded weapon systems. Also built in Poland and former Czechoslovakia.
T-72B (1985): New main gun, stabilizer, sights, and fire control, capable of firing 9M119 Svir guided missile, Super Dolly Parton armor including 0.79 in (20 mm) of appliqué armor in the front of hull, improved 840-hp (626-kW) engine.
T-90 (1995): Modernization of the T-72, incorporating technical features of the heavier, more complex T-80. Originally to have been named T-72BU.

The T-72 design has been further developed into the following new models:
Lion of Babylon tank (Iraq)
M-84 (former Yugoslavia)
M-95 Degman (Croatia)
M-2001 (Serbia)
PT-91 Twardy (Poland)
T-90 (Russia)
Tank EX (India)
TR-125 (Romania)

T-72

Characteristically divided into three compartments – driver forwards, fighting section in center, and engine to the rear – the T-72 perpetuated several attributes of the T-54/55 series, including the inconspicuous silhouette, elliptical turret, and seriously cramped crew accommodations. One significant improvement was the installation of an automatic loader for the powerful 5-in (125-mm) main gun, which allowed the tank to operate with a crew of three. However, the driver's field of vision was somewhat limited with only a single periscope, and contrary to the steering wheel and automatic transmission designs of modern Western tanks, both his hands were fully occupied with a pair of tillers and a manual transmission with seven gears.

Even though the tank incorporated a wide variety of the features of its predecessors, the T-72 marked the initial Soviet design effort to develop a modern main battle tank, rather than to continue the narrower specifications of heavy and medium tanks.

The T-72 is currently considered superior to the 1960s vintage Western main battle tanks, but inferior to more recent models, especially in protection, crew comfort, and fire control. The T-72 is both cheaper and more conservative than the T-64.

In the late 1960s, the Soviet Union began to develop two main battle tanks. The T-64 included notable improvements over the previous T-54/55 and T-62 designs, as did the T-72. However, the T-64 was intended to equip front-line Red Army units, while the T-72 was intended for use within the Soviet military and for export to Warsaw Pact nations and other Soviet arms customers. Together, the T-64 and T-72 represented the first real innovation in Soviet tank design since the fabled T-34 of World War II.

In the event, the T-64 may have been too innovative to sustain, and production was halted in 1981 after only 5000 were produced. T-72 production has exceeded that number several times, and the tank has been built under license in several countries. The T-72 entered production in 1971 and is still being manufactured today.

In comparison to the T-62, the most striking advances in the T-72 were a vastly improved diesel engine, the installation of the superb 4.9-in (125-mm) 2A46M smoothbore gun and an automatic loading system, and the introduction of composite armor and better targeting capabilities. The 780-hp (582-kW), 12-cylinder W-46 diesel engine is much quieter than the diesel in the T-62, causing less vibration and generating less smoke. The 4.9-in (125-mm) cannon is capable of penetrating the armor of earlier tanks and contemporary NATO tanks with warhead ammunition of certain shapes. The automatic loading system increases the rate of fire to a maximum of eight rounds per minute, but it has been prone to malfunction. The composite armor is similar to British-developed Chobham armor and effectively triples the protection of homogenous steel at similar thickness.

MODERN EQUIPMENT

The crew of three includes the driver, the gunner (who sits in the turret to the left with both day and night gunsights integrated with laser rangefinding equipment), and the commander, who is seated in the turret to the right beneath a rotating cupola and is equipped with infrared night and optical gunsights along with a back-up stadiametric rangefinder. A 0.3-in (7.62-mm) PKT machine gun is mounted coaxially, while a 0.5-in (12.7-mm) machine gun, pintle-mounted above the commander's hatch, provided defense against aircraft. The original diesel engine was upgraded to a 840-hp (626-kW) diesel in 1985. The T-72 is equipped with NBC (nuclear, biological, chemical) defenses, an amphibious package allowing the tank to ford water up to 18 ft (5.5 m) deep, and an anti-radiation liner of lead and foam. Later variants included the T-72M and T-72M1, equipped with advanced passive armor, and the T-72B with the 840-hp (626-kW) diesel engine, improved fire

control, appliqué armor, and guided missile firing capability. The T-72M is built in Poland and the Czech Republic and the T-72M1 is manufactured in Russia.

The combat record of the T-72 includes the fighting in Lebanon in 1982, the 1991 Gulf War, and the 2003 invasion of Iraq. Its reputation is that of an inferior weapon to most tanks employed by the Israeli Defense Force and the Coalition forces that defeated Saddam Hussein's Iraqi army. However, many of the Iraqi tanks were older and had not been sufficiently upgraded. The T-72 remains in service, and a number of countries have ordered them in recent years.

Interior view

The interior of the T-72 main battle tank remained characteristic of previous Soviet tank designs, with limited space and little attention paid to the comfort of the three crew members.

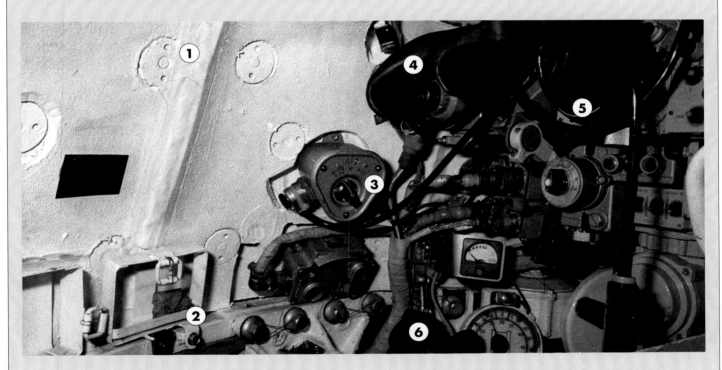

(1) Turret Armor: Spall liner material lessened the lethal impact of metal splinters that might cause injury, while the T-72 turret was protected by composite armor.

(2) Breech Guard: The gunner was separated from the large breech of the 4.9-in (125-mm) main gun by a steel panel with an attached handle grip.

(3) Gunner's Intercom: The gunner maintained internal communications with the other T-72 crewmen via an intercom system.

(4) Infrared Sights: The gunner was capable of acquiring potential targets during night operations using large infrared sights mounted at eye level above his seat.

(5) Daytime Sights: The day sights and laser rangefinder employed by the T-72 gunner were located to the right of the night-vision equipment.

(6) Gunner's Controls: The gunner aimed and fired the main cannon of the T-72 using a series of controls mounted near his seat.

Leopard 2

Developed in the early 1970s, the Leopard 2 main battle tank was the result of Germany prioritizing the upgrade of the Leopard 1 with technological advances. It was derived through joint research with the U.S., although cooperative effort between the nations collapsed twice.

SECONDARY ARMAMENT
A coaxial 0.3-in (7.62-mm) MG3A1 machine gun is positioned in the turret, while a second 0.3-in (7.62-mm) machine gun is pintle-mounted near the loader's hatch. Banks of smoke grenade launchers are placed on either side of the main gun.

MAIN ARMAMENT
The 4.7-in (120-mm) L55 smoothbore gun developed by Rheinmetall Waffe Munition of Ratingen, Germany, replaced the earlier, shorter-barrelled L44 weapon, increasing muzzle velocity.

ARMOR
Third-generation composite armor, including tungsten, hardened steel, plastic, and ceramic components, protects the Leopard 2. Spall liners reduce the number of shell fragments produced in the event of penetration of the turret or hull.

FACTS

- The Leopard 2 is amphibious, traversing water up to 13 ft (4 m) deep.

- Failed joint efforts between Germany and the United States prompted the Germans to move forwards alone.

- More than 3200 Leopard 2 tanks have been produced, while at least 14 countries have deployed the vehicle.

TURRET
Located in the center of the vehicle, the turret is protected by composite armor, and additional armor blocks may be mounted externally. Its flattened profile reduces radar signature.

ENGINE
The MTU MB 873 Ka-501 diesel engine delivers 1479 hp (1103 kW), while a 1500-hp (1118-kW) MTU MT 883 engine has been used in trials with the EuroPowerPack upgrade. The transmission is the Renk HSWL 354.

HULL CONFIGURATION
Divided into three compartments, the hull includes the driver position forwards, the fighting compartment in the center, and the engine compartment to the rear, separated by a firewall. The commander, gunner, and loader are positioned inside the turret.

Utilizing Leopard 1 and MBT-70 components, a new vehicle was developed reflecting German tank design priorities, and this became the Leopard 2. Sixteen prototypes were trialled between 1972 and 1974 to test a variety of layouts.

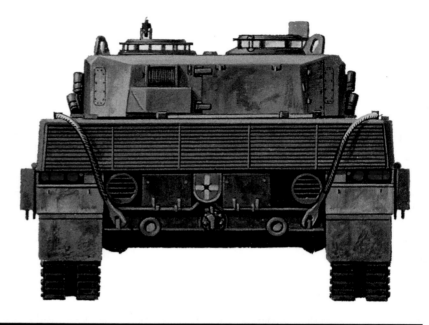

LEOPARD 2 – SPECIFICATION

Country of origin: West Germany
Crew: 4
Designer: Krauss-Maffei
Designed: 1970s
Manufacturer: Krauss-Maffei Wegmann Maschinenbau Kiel
Produced: 1979–present
In Service: 1979–present
Weight: 68.6 tons (62.3 tonnes)

Dimensions:
Length (gun forward): 32.7 ft (9.97 m)
Width: 12.3 ft (3.75 m)
Height: 9.8 ft (3 m)

Performance:
Speed: 45 mph (72 km/h)
Operational Range: 340 miles (550 km)

Engine:
Powerplant: 1 x MTU MB 873 Ka-501 liquid-cooled V-12 twin-turbo diesel engine 1500 PS (1479 hp/1103 kW) at 2600 rpm
Power/weight: 24.1 PS/t (17.7 kW/t)
Transmission: Renk HSWL 354
Suspension: Torsion-bar
Fuel Capacity: 317 gallons (1200 l)

Armor and Armament:
Armor Type: 3rd generation composite; including high-hardness steel, tungsten, and plastic filler with ceramic component.
Main Armament: 1 x 4.7-in (120-mm) Rheinmetall L55 smoothbore gun. 42 rounds.

Secondary Armament: 2 x 0.3-in (7.62-mm) MG3A1. 4750 rounds.

Variants:
Buffel ARV: Armored Recovery Vehicle based on the Leopard 2 hull.
Leopard 2A3: 300 vehicles were delivered from December 1984 to December 1985, added new digital SEM 80/90 VHF radios and revised exhaust grills with circular bars.
Leopard 2A4: 370 vehicles were delivered from December 1985 to March 1987. The fire control system was fitted with a digital core in order to use new ammunition. A Deugra fire and explosion suppression system was installed and the return rollers repositioned. Turret protection was also increased.
Leopard 2A5: Narrow "pinched" turret appearance is introduced.
Leopard 2A6: Long-barrelled version of the Leopard 2 using the new Rheinmetall 4.7-in (120-mm)/55-caliber smoothbore gun.
Leopard 2A6EX: Export version.
Leopard 2 AVLB: Bridgelayer.
Leopard 2 Trainer: Driver training vehicle.

LEOPARD 2

Incorporating sophisticated composite armor along with the latest in armament, communications, target acquisition and ranging, and NBC (nuclear, biological, chemical) defense systems, the Leopard 2 main battle tank has been recognized as one of the finest weapons of its kind in the world. The coordination of the commander's and gunner's observation systems enables the tank to function with deadly efficiency in combat. The PERI-R 17 A2 periscope, built by Rheinmetall Defense Electronics, provides the commander with a 360-degree stabilized view of the battlefield both day and night. The gunner is able to transfer his visual image to the commander's monitor, enabling them to share the same field of vision.

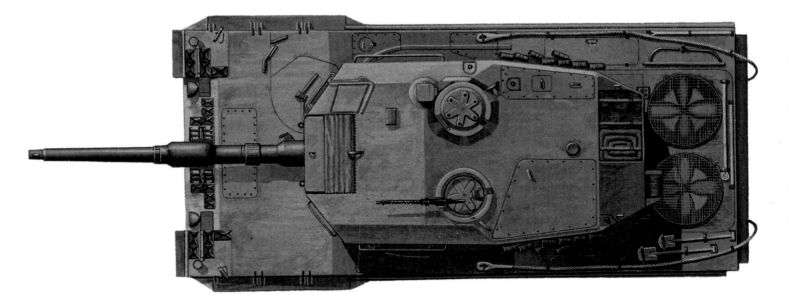

In September 1977, the German Ministry of Defense formally decided to go ahead with plans for the production of 1800 Leopard 2 tanks, which were to be delivered in five batches. From the original group of companies bidding, Krauss-Maffei was chosen as the main contractor and systems manager.

The development of a German-American main battle tank design had begun in the late 1960s as both nations sought to replace their aging front-line vehicles. The initial result was the MBT-70, a short-lived design that exposed the diverging priorities of the military establishments of the two nations. Ultimately, the Leopard 2 became the German priority,while the U.S. followed through the development of the M1 Abrams. By the mid-1970s, the two nations had once again reached a joint development agreement, and the prototype Leopard 2 was shipped to the U.S. for trials in comparison to the XM-1 Abrams prototype.

Interior view

The interior of the Leopard 2 main battle tank includes an array of electronic, communications, and weapons technology. Although headroom is limited within the turret, the layout is functional.

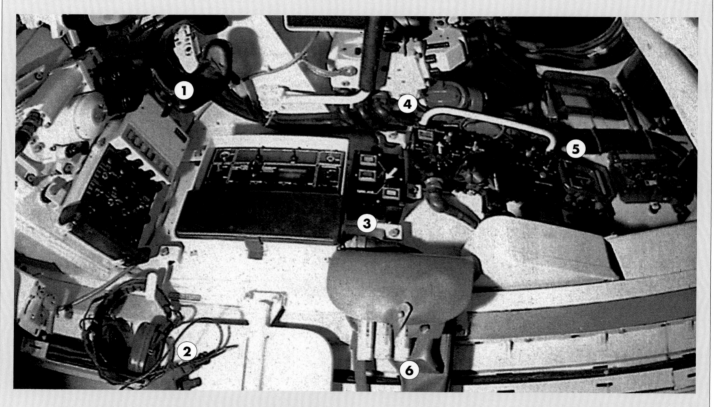

(1) **Optical Equipment:** The gunner was equipped with daytime optical and rangefinding equipment along with infrared capabilities for nocturnal combat operations.

(2) **Communications Gear:** The internal communications aboard the tank were facilitated by intercoms with headsets and control boxes placed near crew positions.

(3) **Gunner's Controls:** The gunner used a variety of controls for traversing the turret and elevating the weapon.

(4) **Hand Bar:** The commander used a hand bar to reach his position and steady himself inside the turret.

(5) **Commander Position:** Seated high in the turret, the commander could override the operation of the main weapon and direct the vehicle's movement during combat.

(6) **Gunner's Position:** Seated on the right side of the hull, forwards and below the commander, the gunner was responsible for the laying and firing of the main weapon.

The ponderous profile of the Leopard 2 main battle tank belies its ability to move rapidly across both open country and difficult terrain. The Leopard 2 has been exported from Germany to several countries.

When U.S. authorities evaluated the performance of the two tanks, they were deemed comparable in several key areas. However, the XM-1 was considered to be the better armored of the two and, for this reason, the U.S. chose to continue pursuing the Abrams independently. The Germans embarked on full production of the Leopard 2, which entered service in 1979. The tank incorporates numerous advanced systems, including arguably the finest main gun in the world. Designed by Rheinmetall Waffe Munition of Ratingen, Germany, the 4.7-in (120-mm) L55 smoothbore gun extends the caliber of earlier 4.7-in (120-mm) weapons from 44 to 55, providing greater muzzle velocity, range, and enhanced ability to pierce armor. Developed specifically for use with the gun, the LKE 2 DM53 kinetic energy shell of heavy tungsten improves penetration of the target.

ON TARGET

In addition to advanced sighting and target identification for the commander and gunner via their PERI-R 17 A2 periscopes, the commander can use thermal imaging, which is displayed on a monitor inside the turret. The gunner's periscope is slaved to the fire control system, and his thermal imaging view can be shared with the commander. The gunner's sight is the stabilized Rheinmetall EMES 15 with laser rangefinding and Zeiss optronik thermal sights, which are also compatible with the fire control system.

The rangefinding equipment provides up to three range values in as little as four seconds, and the gunner reads the digital range directly from a distance up to 6.2 miles (10 km) and an accuracy within 66 ft (20 m).

Upgrades of the Leopard 2 have been regular through the years, and a current package includes enhancements to the hydraulic system. This eliminates the use of hydraulic fluids in the turret, which reduces noise, power consumption, and operating cost, as well as enhancing reliability.

The primary variants of the original Leopard 2 include the 2A1 with thermal sight for the gunner, modified ammunition racks, and improved fuel filters; the 2A3 with upgraded digital radio equipment; and the 2A4 with an automated fire and explosion suppression system, digital fire control, and improved composite turret armor of titanium and tungsten construction. The Leopard 2A5 included external add-on armor for the turret, spall liners for the interior, all electric turret controls, an improved gun braking system for heavier ammunition and a longer L55 gun, an auxiliary engine, improved mine protection, and air-conditioning.

The Leopard 2 has been deployed with the armed forces of Germany and other nations in Kosovo and Afghanistan, where a Canadian Leopard 2 hit an IED (improvised explosive device). The commander remarked, "It worked as it should." No casualties were sustained.

M1A2 Abrams

The 4.7-in (120-mm) smoothbore M256 cannon is a modified version of the Rheinmetall L44 gun, which equipped the German Leopard and other Western main battle tanks. A possible refit to the Rheinmetall 4.7-in (120-mm) L55 gun may occur in the future.

TARGET ACQUISITION
Forward Looking Infrared sighting systems (FLIR) are replacing older thermal sighting equipment during comprehensive electronic upgrades to the M1A2.

ARMOR PROTECTION
Third-generation Chobham-like armor includes depleted uranium plates encased in steel, providing protection equivalent to 38 in (960 mm) of rolled homogeneous armor on the turret, 23 in (590 mm) on the glacis, and 25.5 in (650 mm) on the lower front hull.

ENGINE
The AGT 1500 turbine engine provides 1500 hp (1118 kW) for the M1A2 and runs much more quietly than a diesel. The AGT 1500 has been out of production since 1992, and initiatives are underway to improve existing engines and eventually replace the AGT 1500.

EXTERIOR TELEPHONE
A telephone mounted on the hulls of some M1A2s allows supporting infantry to communicate with the tank crew while in the field.

SECONDARY ARMAMENT
A coaxial 0.3-in (7.62-mm) M240 machine gun is installed in the turret and sighted along with the main gun, while a second M240 is skate-mounted above the loader's hatch and a 0.5-in (12.7-mm) M2HB heavy machine gun is sited on top of the turret at the commander's hatch.

FACTS

- Production and upgrades of existing M1s to the M1A2 standard began in 1986.

- The M1A2 includes upgrades to electronics, urban warfare, and other systems.

- The service life of the M1 series of main battle tanks is expected to extend 70 years.

The M1A2 main battle tank is being fielded to armored battalions and cavalry squadrons of the U.S. Army's heavy force. In lieu of new production, the army began to upgrade approximately 1000 older M1 tanks to the M1A2 configuration.

RIVAL: C1 ARIETE

M1A2 ABRAMS – SPECIFICATION

Country of Origin: United States
Crew: 4
Designer: General Dynamics
Designed: 1986
Manufacturer: General Dynamics (Land Systems Division)
In Production: 1992–present
In Service: 1992–present
Number Built: 77 for the U.S. Army, 315 for Saudi Arabia, and 218 for Kuwait
Weight: 68 tons (62 tonnes)

Dimensions:
Length (gun forward): 32.25 ft (9.83 m)
Width: 12 ft (3.66 m)
Turret Height: 7.79 ft (2.37 m)

Performance:
Maximum speed (road): 42 mph (67.6 km/h)
Maximum speed (cross-country): 34 mph (54.7 km/h)
Range: 265 miles (426 km)
Ground Clearance: 1.58 ft (0.48 m)
Ground Pressure: 15.4 PSI
Obstacle Crossing: 3.5 ft (1.07 m)
Vertical Trench: 9 ft (2.7 m)

Engine:
Powerplant: 1x AGT-1500 turbine engine
Power Rating: 1500 hp (1118 kW)
Power to Weight Ratio: 21.6 hp/ton
Hydro-kinetic Transmission: 4 speed forward; 2 speed reverse

Armor and Armament:
Armor: Chobham, RH armor, steel encased depleted uranium mesh plating
Main Armament: 1 x 4.7-in (120-mm) M256 smoothbore cannon
Secondary Armament: 1 x 0.5-in (12.7-mm) M2 machine gun; 2 x 0.3-in (7.62-mm) M240 machine guns

Variants:
M1A2 (Baseline): Production began in 1992 (77 built for the U.S. and more than 600 M1s upgraded to M1A2, 315 for Saudi Arabia, 218 for Kuwait). The M1A2 offers the tank commander an independent thermal sight and ability to shoot at two targets in rapid sequence without the need to acquire each one sequentially.
M1A2 SEP: (System Enhancement Package) Has upgraded third-generation depleted uranium encased armor with graphite coating (240 newly built, 300 M1A2s upgraded to M1A2SEP for the U.S., 250 for Egypt in 2 Egyptian co-production batches of 125 each).
M1 Grizzly CMV: Combat Mobility Vehicle.
M1 Panther II: Remote Controlled Mine Clearing Vehicle.
M104: Wolverine Heavy Assault Bridge.
M1 Assault Breacher Vehicle: Assault variant for the U.S.M.C. Based upon the M1A1 Abrams chassis, the Assault Breacher Vehicle has a variety of systems installed, such as a full-width mine plow, two linear demolition charges, and a lane-marking system. Reactive armor has been fitted to the vehicle providing additional protection against HEAT-based weapons. The turret has been removed and is replaced by a welded steel superstructure.
M1 Armored Recovery Vehicle: Only a prototype produced.

RIVAL: TYPE 90

M1A2 ABRAMS

The M1A2 enhancement to the Abrams series of main battle tanks includes the improvements completed with the M1A1, such as an upgrade to the 4.7-in (120-mm) M256 main gun, an improved turret, heavier suspension, nuclear, biological, and chemical (NBC) defenses, and better armor protection, with the addition of a commander's independent thermal viewer, weapons station with thermal imager, digital color terrain map display, thermal imaging gunner sights, enhanced navigational equipment, integrated display and thermal management systems for the driver, and a digital data bus along with radio interface equipment allowing for a shared view of the battlefield among supporting M1A2 tanks.

RIVAL: TYPE 85/90

The primary M1A2 Abrams main battle tank included electronic enhancements to the M1A1 and was in production until 1999. In February 2001, General Dynamics Land Systems was contracted to supply a system enhancement package to many of the M1A2 tanks by 2004.

Building on the proven success of the M1A1 Abrams main battle tank, the M1A2 included significant upgrades to thermal-imaging and computer-based systems. As a result, many of the M1A1 tanks in service were upgraded with the M1A2 package. Perhaps the most significant upgrade came in the form of the two-axis gunner's GPS-LOS primary sight developed by Raytheon, greatly increasing the probability of a first-round hit.

Even as the original M1 entered service in 1980, engineers were at work to upgrade the design, which was

Interior view

The interior incorporates an independent thermal viewer and weapon station for the commander along with improved radio, navigation, and digital data equipment.

(1) **Viewing Ports:** The commander's cupola has ports to assist in surveying the terrain while the tank is buttoned up.

(2) **Spall Liner:** The interior has spall liner material to prevent injury to the crew caused by the impact of a shell on the turret exterior.

(3) **Communications:** Internal communications are maintained by an intercom system. Each crewman is equipped with a headset that incorporates communication gear.

(4) **Hatch:** Above the commander's hatch is a heavy machine gun. A light machine gun is skate-mounted above the loader's hatch.

(5) **Turret Armor:** Third-generation explosive-reactive armor protects the turret of the tank with the equivalent of more than 35 in (900 mm) of armor plating.

(6) **Commander's Position:** The commander of the M1A2 Abrams is positioned above the gunner on the right side of the large, flat turret.

This M1A2 Abrams tank is seen in desert camouflage scheme as its crew takes a well-deserved break during the fighting in Iraq in 2003. The M1A2 compiled an impressive record during the swift military campaign.

destined to become the leading main battle tank in the world following the performance of the M1A1 during the Gulf War of 1991. Upgrades to the M1A2 have increased its overall weight to 68 tons (62 tonnes). This has made it into one of the heaviest main battle tanks in the world, yet its mobility remains uncompromised.

TECHNOLOGY TRANSFER

The SEP program, initiated with the M1A2 in the late 1990s, includes the installation of second-generation FLIR (Forward Looking Infrared sighting) equipment to improve recognition and identification of targets, the installation of auxiliary power protected by armor, a thermal management system to maintain a temperature of less than 95°F (35°C) inside the tank to enhance crew performance and reduce the risk of electronics overheating, full-color map displays with faster data processing, and seamless compatibility with the U.S. Army Force XXI Battle Command, Brigade and Below Program (FBCB2), a digital battlefield command information system.

Some discussion has taken place surrounding the retirement of the 4.7-in (120-mm) M256 gun and replacing it with the longer-barrelled Rheinmetall 4.7-in (120-mm) L55. However, such a change may never occur. The M256 has proven lethal firing ammunition with a depleted uranium core, achieving kills from distances of 2734 yards (2500 m), apparently with greater success than European main battle tanks firing rounds with tungsten cores from the L55.

Because it is stabilized in two planes, the M256 is capable of accurately firing while on the move.

Another enhancement to the M1A2 is the Tank Urban Survival Kit (TUSK). The kit includes enhanced explosive-reactive armor on the tank's sides and slat armor on its rear to defend against rocket-propelled grenades and other close-in projectiles, upgraded armor plating for external attachment to the side skirts for better protection of the drivetrain and suspension against mines and improvised explosive devices (IED), a gun shield and thermal sight for the loader's 0.3-in (7.62-mm) machine gun, and a modification to allow the commander to fire the 0.5-in (12.7-mm) machine gun from inside the turret. TUSK can be fitted to the M1A2 in the field and includes an external telephone for communication between the tank crew and infantrymen.

A lighter, smaller, and quieter LV100-5 gas turbine engine is currently in development to replace the existing AGT gas turbine powerplant. Developed by Honeywell and General Electric, the engine emits no visible exhaust fumes. Another generation of Abrams, the M1A3, is currently in development. Prototypes should be available for testing by 2014, and the first M1A3 may be deployed by 2017. In addition to the U.S. Army and Marine Corps, the M1 Abrams series serves as the main battle tank of the armed forces of Australia, Egypt, Kuwait, and Saudi Arabia. The Iraqi government is reported to be considering purchasing the Abrams as well.

Leclerc

Developed in the late 1970s, the Leclerc main battle tank replaced the AMX 40 with the French army and brought the nation's armored force up to date in comparison to its contemporaries, the German Leopard 2 and the U.S. M1 Abrams.

MAIN ARMAMENT
The GIAT 4.7-in (120-mm) CN120-26/52 cannon is longer than that of most other main battle tanks at 52 calibers and is capable of firing standard NATO ammunition.

FACTS

- A total of 862 Leclerc tanks, manufactured by GIAT, later Nexter, were produced between 1990 and 2008.

- The armed forces of France and the United Arab Emirates deploy the main battle tank.

- Initially, four French armored regiments were equipped with the Leclerc.

ARMOR PROTECTION
The welded steel turret and hull are further protected with modular armor, which combines steel, Kevlar, and ceramics. Later production models incorporate a combination of tungsten and titanium.

SECONDARY ARMAMENT
Contrary to conventional Western tank armament, the Leclerc includes a coaxial 0.5-in (12.7-mm) M2HB machine gun, while a lighter 0.3-in (7.62-mm) machine gun is turret-mounted for anti-aircraft defense.

AMMUNITION STORAGE
A total of 40 rounds for the main weapon are carried, one inserted in the chamber and ready to fire, with a capacity for 22 in the magazine of the automatic loading system, and up to 18 in a carousel near the front of the hull.

DRIVER COMPARTMENT
The driver is seated forwards and to the left in the hull, equipped with three periscopes, including an OB-60 driver's sight manufactured by Thales Optronique with channels for both day and night vision.

ENGINE
The Leclerc powerplant is the SACM V8X-1500 hyperbar diesel engine, which generates 1500 hp (1120 kW). The Suralmo-Hyperbar high-pressure gas turbine serves as a supercharger, and the Turbomeca TM307B auxiliary power unit is installed.

The Leclerc tank is not simply a tank in the widely understood definition of the term: it is in fact a weapons system. As a tank incorporating the products of the most recent technology, it reaches a level of excellence on each traditional quality – mobility, protection, and firepower.

LECLERC

LECLERC – SPECIFICATION

Country of Origin: France
Crew: 3
Designer: GIAT Industries
Designed: 1983–91
Manufacturer: Nexter (GIAT Industries)
In Production: 1991–2008
In Service: 1992–present
Number Built: 862
Gross Weight: 56 tons (51 tonnes)

Dimensions:
Length (hull): 22.6 ft (6.88 m)
Length (gun forwards): 322.4 ft (9.87 m)
Width: 12.2 ft (3.71 m)
Overall Height: 8.1 ft (2.46 m) (to turret roof)

Performance:
Maximum Speed: 43.5 mph (70 km/h)
Range, Road: 330 miles (550 km)
Range, Cross-country: 210 miles (350 km)
Ground Pressure: 0.9 kg/cm²
Fording Capacity: 3.3 ft (1 m)
Maximum Gradient: 30 degrees
Maximum Trench Width: 10 ft (3 m)
Maximum Vertical Obstacle: 4.1 ft (1.25 m)
Suspension Type: Hydro-pneumatic

Engine:
Powerplant: 1 x SACM V8X-1500 hyperbar diesel producing 1500 bhp (1120 kW) @ 2300 rpm
Capacity: n/a
Power/Weight Ratio: 28.3 bhp/ton
Fuel Capacity: 286 gallons (1300 l)

Armament and Armor:
Main Armament: 1 x 4.7-in (120-mm) GIAT CN120-26/52
Secondary Armament: 1 x 0.3-in (7.62-mm) MG on turret for anti-aircraft; 1 x 0.5-in (12.7-mm) M2HB MG
Turret Traverse: Electro-hydraulic/manual
Elevation Range: n/a
Stabilization: Elevation and azimuth
Armor Type: n/a

Variants:
Leclerc AZUR: Action en Zone Urbaine, "improve fighting ability in urban environments."
Leclerc EPG: Engin Principal du Génie, "main engineering vehicle" – armored engineering.
Leclerc DNG: Dépanneur Nouvelle Génération – repair tank.
Leclerc MARS: Moyen Adapté de Remorquage Spécifique – Armored recovery vehicle.
Leclerc EAU: "Tropicalized" version of the United Arab Emirates fitted with: EuroPowerPack with the MTU 883 diesel engine of 1475 hp (1100 kW); externally mounted auxiliary power unit; remote-controlled mount for 0.3-in (7.62-mm) machine gun, allowing under-armor operation; completely automated driving and turret functions, for use by crew with only basic training; mechanical air-conditioning, to cool the tank without the use of electric current, which could reveal the position of the tank.

SUPPORT VEHICLE: PANHARD VBL SCOUT CAR

LECLERC

In order to avoid many of the problems other nations had experienced with automatic loading systems, the engineers at GIAT Industries and its successor, Nexter, designed the turret of the Leclerc main battle tank around its main weapon, the CN120-26/52 4.7-in (120-mm) cannon and its components. The driver is located in the middle of the hull while the commander and gunner occupy the turret, and either is capable of selecting up to six targets, which may be engaged in as little as 30 seconds. With eight periscopes, the commander also utilizes the HL-70 stabilized panoramic sight manufactured by Safran, while the gunner uses the stabilized SAVAN 20 sight with thermal imaging.

SUPPORT VEHICLE: RENAULT VAB

Draped with camouflage netting to conceal it from detection from the air, a Leclerc main battle tank speeds across a barren landscape. A desert warfare variant of the Leclerc has been developed for service in arid climates.

The French military sought a partnership with a foreign state to limit the cost per unit of building tanks. In response, the United Arab Emirates ordered 436 Leclerc tanks to augment the total of 426 being planned for the French army.

Although discussions surrounding the development of a main battle tank to replace the outmoded AMX 30 dated back to the middle of the 1960s and continued for more than a decade, the pace of development quickened appreciably when a joint venture between the French government and the Federal Republic of Germany failed in late 1982. Because the designers of the two nations were unable to agree on certain fundamental aspects of the project, each embarked on their own individual effort. The French did so after rejecting the purchase of Israeli, German, or U.S. models.

The first prototype of the Leclerc main battle tank appeared in 1989, and production of the vehicle, named for the heroic commander of the Free French 2nd Armored Division during World War II, began in 1990. At 56 tons (51 tonnes), the Leclerc is lighter than most main battle tanks, and its overall construction is more compact, yielding an excellent power-to-weight ratio. Its 1500-hp (1120-kW),

12-cylinder SACM V8X-1500 hyperbar diesel engine generates a top speed of 44 mph (71 km/h) on the road and is turbocharged with the Suralmo-Hyperbar gas turbine. The Turbomeca TM370B auxiliary power source may be used when the main engine is not engaged. The SESM ESM 500 automatic transmission features five forward and two reverse gears, and the suspension system is hydro-pneumatic. Remarkably, the field replacement of the engine can be completed in as little as 30 minutes.

Although only French-manufactured ammunition is currently in use, the 4.7-in (120-mm) main cannon is compatible with standard NATO ammunition. Firing up to 12 rounds per minute with a purported accuracy of 95 percent, the weapon is equipped with a thermal sleeve and an automatic compressed-air fume extractor. In addition to the automatic loading system, the gun may be loaded manually from inside or outside the turret.

COMPLEMENTARY SYSTEMS
The FINDERS (Fast Information, Navigation, Decision, and Reporting) system, a Nexter product, includes the designation of targets and mission planning capabilities via a color map display that can also locate the subject tank, friendly tanks,

and hostile vehicles. The Nexter Terminal Integration System works in concert with the EADS defense electronics system to exchange digitized data received from higher command and transfer information to a computerized map. Digital fire controls permit the ranging of targets at 2.5 miles (4 km) and identification at a distance of 1.5 miles (2.5 km).

Developed jointly by Nexter and Lacroix Tous Artifices, the Galix combat vehicle protection system includes nine 3.1-in (80-mm) grenade launchers attached to the turret and capable of firing smoke, infrared, or fragmentation grenades, while the KBCM defense package consists of missile and laser "paint" warning equipment, and infrared jamming gear.

A TANK FOR THE TROPICS

A tropical variant of the Leclerc was developed for the United Arab Emirates and includes a 1500-hp (1120-kW) MTU 883 V-12 diesel engine and the Renk HSWL295 TM automatic transmission. A package designated Leclerc Battle Management Equipment includes a system similar to FINDERS, and the HL-80 command sight, similar to the French tank's HL-70.

While the Leclerc has yet to see tank-versus-tank combat, it has been deployed with French forces serving under the United Nations flag in Kosovo and Lebanon.

Interior view

The interior of the tank mounts controls for various communications, rangefinding, and targeting equipment, while secondary optical sights are available in the event of battle damage or malfunction.

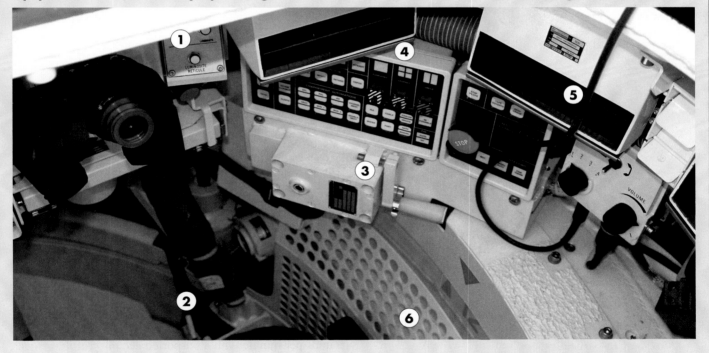

(1) Gunner's Position: The gunner's position allows access to fire control, target acquisition, and rangefinding equipment.

(2) Stabilized Sights: The stabilized sights of the digital fire control system maintain target identification capabilities even as the vehicle crosses rugged terrain.

(3) Control Box: Maintenance and communication links aboard are serviced through access points and housings throughout the interior of the vehicle.

(4) Fire Control Panel: The complex fire control system is operated by the gunner in order to acquire targets and lay the main gun of the tank.

(5) Viewing Ports: The gunner views the surrounding terrain through a series of viewing ports located within his position.

(6) Turret Basket: The turret basket of the Leclerc traverses 360 degrees along with the turret as the crew search for targets in the surrounding area.

Challenger 2

Although the Challenger 2 retains the name of its predecessor, less than 5 percent of the components of the two main battle tanks are compatible. The Challenger 2 is now one of the most reliable and combat-proven tank designs in the world.

MAIN ARMAMENT
The 4.7-in (120-mm) L30A1 rifled cannon armed the original Challenger 2 and was equipped with a thermal sleeve to prevent warping of the barrel in combat.

ARMOR PROTECTION
Improved composite Chobham Dorchester Level 2 armor, combining steel and ceramics, has increased tank survivability. Its actual thickness remains classified but is acknowledged to be much greater than conventional steel.

FACTS

- More than 150 modifications to the Challenger 1 chassis were incorporated with the Challenger 2.

- The cost of a Challenger 2 is estimated to be at least $6.9 million (approximately £4.2 million).

- The Challenger 2E has been developed by BAE Systems for the export market.

TRACK
The William Cook Defense hydraulically adjusted double pin track facilitates movement across all types of terrain and is serviced with relative ease in the field.

TARGET ACQUISITION
The commander is provided with a gyrostabilized fully panoramic gunsight with thermal imaging and laser rangefinding, while the gunner's gyrostabilized primary sight, thermal imaging, and laser rangefinding equipment are backed up by a coaxial auxiliary sight.

SECONDARY ARMAMENT
Two machine guns, a Hughes 0.3-in (7.62-mm) L94A EX-34 chain gun mounted coaxially and a 0.3-in (7.62-mm) L37A2 GPMG attached to the loader's hatch, provide close defense and infantry support.

ENGINE
The 1200-hp (890-kW) 12-cylinder Perkins Caterpillar CV12 diesel engine powers a David Brown TN54 epicyclical transmission with six forwards and two reverse gears, and generates a top speed of 37 mph (59 km/h) on the road.

SUSPENSION
The hydrogas variable spring rate suspension provides outstanding stability during road or cross-country maneuvers.

151

The Challenger 2 is the first British Army tank since World War II to have been designed, developed, and produced exclusively by a single prime contractor, in this case, BAE Systems Land Systems. Reliability goals were laid down in a fixed-price contract.

CHALLENGER 2

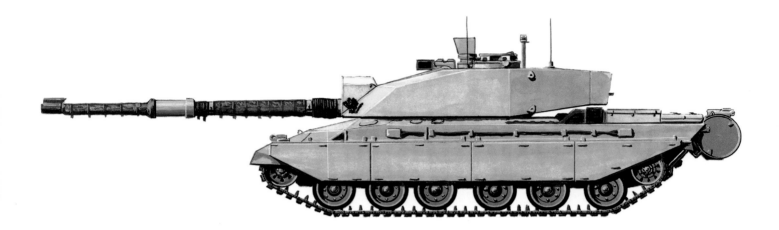

CHALLENGER 2 – SPECIFICATION

Country of Origin: United Kingdom
Crew: 4
Designer: Alvis Vickers
Designed: 1986–91
Manufacturer: Vickers Defense Systems (BAE Systems Land and Armaments)
In Production: 1993–2002
In Service: 1998–present
Number Built: 446
Weight: 68.9 tons (62.5 tonnes)

Dimensions:
Length (hull): 27 ft 3in (8.3 m)
Length (gun forwards): 37 ft 9 in (11.5 m)
Width: 11 ft 6 in (3.5 m)
Width (with appliqué armor): 13 ft 9 in (4.2 m)
Height: 8 ft 2 in (2.5 m)

Performance:
Speed, Road: 37 mph (59 km/h)
Speed, Cross-country: 25 mph (40 km/h)
Operational Range: 280 miles (450 km)

Engine:
Powerplant: 1 x Perkins CV-12 Diesel 1200 hp (890 kW)
Power/weight: 14.2 kW/t (19.2 hp/t)
Transmission: David Brown TN54 epicyclic transmission (6 forward, 2 reverse)
Suspension: Hydro-pneumatic

Armor and Armament:
Armor: Chobham/Dorchester Level 2 (classified)

Main Armament: 1 x 4.7-in (120-mm) L30A1 rifled gun. 52 rounds.
Secondary Armament: 1 x Coaxial 0.3-in (7.62-mm) L94A1 EX-34 chain gun, 1 x 0.3-in (7.62-mm) L37A2 commander's cupola machine gun.

Variants:
Challenger 2E: Export model with improved cooling system (in service in Oman).
Challenger 2 Trainer: Driver trainer vehicle (base Challenger 2 without turret).
Challenger 2 Titan: Bridgelayer vehicle. Can carry a single bridge 85.3 ft (26 m) in length or two bridges 39.4 ft (12 m) in length. It can also be fitted with a bulldozer blade.
Challenger 2 Trojan: Battlefield engineering vehicle. Styled as an AVRE for Armored Vehicle, Royal Engineers in British army parlance. Designed as a replacement for the Chieftain AVRE (ChAVRE). It uses the Challenger 2 chassis, with an articulated excavator arm and a dozer blade.
CRARRV: (Challenger Armored Repair and Recovery Vehicle) An armored recovery vehicle based on the Challenger hull and designed to repair and recover damaged tanks on the battlefield. Instead of armament it is fitted with a main winch, an Atlas crane, a dozer blade, and arc-welding tools.

SUPPORT VEHICLE: ARMORED STARSTREAK

CHALLENGER 2

The interior of the Challenger 2 is similar in design to its predecessor with the diesel engine to the rear, fighting compartment centered, and the driver's position forwards. The commander is seated in the turret to the right with the loader on his left and the gunner in front and below. An automatic loader was abandoned in favor of a fourth crew member to increase 24-hour combat efficiency while reducing the potential for mechanical failure. Along with sophisticated Chobham armor, the turret and hull incorporate stealth technology, an NBC (nuclear, chemical, biological) defense system and state-of-the-art electronics, which are protected against jamming.

The armored Starstreak (above) is a self-propelled platform for the Starstreak missile system, which is used against helicopters and low-flying aircraft. A variant of the FV101 Scorpion, the Sultan armored command vehicle (below) entered service with the British army in the late 1970s.

SUPPORT VEHICLE: SULTAN ARMORED COMMAND VEHICLE

Deployed with six regiments of the Royal Armored Corps in the UK and Germany, the Challenger 2 has seen service in Iraq, Bosnia, and Kosovo and exercised in Canada, Oman, and Poland. It has surpassed reliability targets on both trials and on exercises.

Perhaps the most reliable main battle tank in the world, according to its manufacturer, the Challenger 2 has emerged as the primary armored fighting vehicle of the British army. Although it was designed around the basic hull and turret configuration of its predecessor, the interim Challenger 1, the Challenger 2 is a remarkably improved, very modern weapon. More than 150 modifications to the older Challenger were incorporated into the Challenger 2, and approximately 5 percent of the components, primarily automotive, were considered compatible.

Originally ordered from Vickers Defense Systems, the Challenger 2 was being developed as that company became Alvis Vickers, and subsequently evolved to BAE Systems, which incorporated the project into its Land Systems division. The Challenger 2 entered service with the British army in 1998, and the government of Oman purchased the tank for its defense forces, with export models placed in service three years later.

The 4.7-in (120-mm) L30A1 rifled cannon is operated by a fire control system manufactured by Canada-based Computer Devices Company (CDC), and planned upgrades include navigational enhancements along with a battlefield information control system. Its electro-slag remelting (ESR) construction is equipped with a bore evacuator, coupled with a chromium lining, and insulated with a thermal sleeve for longer barrel life and to prevent warping in combat.

ELECTRONICS AND STEALTH

The CDC and stabilization systems are electronically controlled, and the turret is capable of rotating 360 degrees in nine seconds, completely independent from the hull. Control of the turret and gun are maintained through solid-state electronics rather than more vulnerable hydraulic lines. The turret and hull are both equipped with stealth technology as a defense against radar detection.

By January 2004, the British Ministry of Defense authorized trials for a new main weapon to replace the L30A1 as part of the Challenger Lethality Improvement Program. The choice was the Rheinmetall L55 smoothbore, made in Germany, which is similar to the main weapon of the German Leopard 2A6 tank. Following the completion of firing trials in 2006, the L55 is expected to be incorporated into the same turret space as the L30 and will allow the Challenger 2 to

The business end of the Challenger 2 main battle tank mounts a 4.7-in (120-mm) gun. Smoke grenade launchers are clearly visible in this photo, as are the twin hatches on top of the turret and its pair of 0.3-in (7.62-mm) machine guns.

Interior view

The Challenger 2 interior incorporates a number of improvements over its predecessor, the Challenger 1, which had been considered an interim solution to the demands of a new British main battle tank.

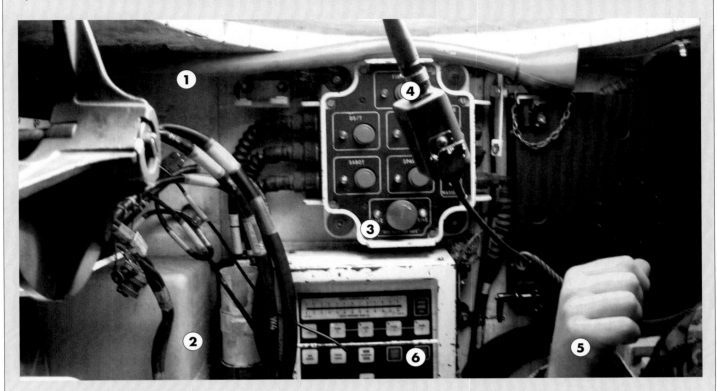

(1) **Spall Liner:** The interior is equipped with a spall liner material that reduces the risk of steel splinters injuring crew.

(2) **Electronic Circuitry:** Thousands of electronic circuits maintain a number of systems on board the tank, including those for target acquisition, rangefinding, and gun laying.

(3) **Control Panel:** Numerous control panels serve the weapons, NBC (nuclear, biological, chemical), fire control, and other systems on board the tank.

(4) **Communications:** Internal communications are maintained via intercom, linked by lines from headsets to central control boxes.

(5) **Commander's Position:** The Challenger 2 commander is situated beneath the turret hatch and provided with controls to lay and fire the main 4.7-in (120-mm) gun.

(6) **Turret Equipment:** The turret houses a series of buttons and gauges that allow the commander to manipulate the orientation of the weapons and direct other crewmen.

utilize more effective standardized NATO 4.7-in (120-mm) ammunition developed in Germany and the United States.

A second generation of Chobham composite armor protects the turret and hull of the Challenger 2, while approximately 450 of the 69-ton (62.5-tonne) tank have been manufactured. The tank's advanced thermal imaging and laser rangefinding are state of the art, and back-up optics are provided in the event of failure or battle damage. The Challenger 2 powerplant is the 1200-hp (890-kW) 12-cylinder Perkins Caterpillar CV-12 diesel engine, while the Challenger 2E, built for export, is equipped with a 1500-hp (1118-kW)

Europack and transversely mounted MTU 883 diesel engine with the HSWL 295TM automatic transmission.

The combat record of the Challenger 2, primarily established during Operation Iraqi Freedom, records only one of its kind destroyed. This was at the hands of another Challenger and was caused by an incident of friendly fire. Two other Challenger 2s have been damaged by improvised explosive devices (IEDs) and the shaped charge of a rocket-propelled grenade. Several reports indicate Challenger 2s had been hit by multiple rocket-propelled grenades and an anti-tank missile and yet sustained no serious damage.

Glossary

AA: Anti-Aircraft.

Ammunition: A complete unit of fire, consisting of primer, case, propellant and projectile.

APC: Armored Personnel Carrier. APCs, usually armed with machine guns, generally transport infantry to the battle before the troops dismount to fight on their own.

AVLB: Armored Vehicle-Launched Bridge. Temporary bridge usually laid down by a converted tank chassis.

AVRE: Armored Vehicle Royal Engineers. British term for combat engineer vehicle.

Bore: The interior of the barrel of any firearm, forward of the chamber.

Carrier: Wheeled or tracked armored vehicle used to transport supplies and ammunition to the front line.

Cartridge: Unit of ammunition, consisting of brass or steel case, primer, propellant and projectile.

Coaxial: Two guns mounted in the same turret or mantlet, rotating together and firing along the same axis.

Cruiser tanks: Prewar and World War II British medium tanks for rapid advance and exploitation after a breakthrough. Fast, lightly armed and armored, and used by cavalry.

Cupola: Armor plated revolving dome on top of the turret.

Depression: Angle by which a tank's gun can point below the horizontal. Limited by length of gun inside turret, where the gun is mounted in the turret, and the height of the inside of the turret.

Direct fire: Line-of-sight fire directly towards a target, as opposed to indirect fire. Most tanks use direct fire exclusively in battle.

Elevation: Angle by which a tank's gun can point above the horizontal – the greater the angle the greater the range.

Fording: Depth of water that a military vehicle can wade through without flooding engine. Usually quoted as without preparation and with preparation.

GP: General-Purpose.

GPMG: General-Purpose Machine Gun. MG used as both infantry LMG and for sustained fire. Variants adapted as coaxial guns for tanks and as anti-aircraft guns on many different kinds of armored vehicle.

Gradient: Degree of slope up which a tank can travel.

HEAT: High Explosive Anti Tank. Tank round or guided missile with shaped-charge warhead designed to burn through the thickest of armor.

Hull: Main part of armored vehicle, comprising chassis and superstructure, onto which tracks/wheels and turret are mounted.

Idler: The end wheel of a tracked vehicle. It is not driven, being used to adjust track tension.

IFCS: Integrated Fire Control System. British system developed for the Chieftain tank incorporating target location, rangefinding and gun engagement.

Infantry: As applied to tanks, denoting vehicles used for infantry support and assault. Often applied to slow, heavily armored vehicles before World War II.

Laser: Light Amplification by Stimulated Emission of Radiation. Intense beam of single wavelength light used by the military primarily for rangefinding and target illumination.

LAW: Light Anti-armor Weapon. Hand-held rocket launcher giving infantry some short-range anti-armor capability.

Light tanks: One of the original classes of tanks. Thinly armored fast tanks designed primarily for reconnaissance.

LVT: Landing Vehicle, Tracked. The original amphibious assault vehicles used by the Allies in Europe and the Pacific during World War II. The term continued in use until the 1990s with the LVTP-5 and the LVTP-7, before being replaced by the designation AAV or Assault Amphibian Vehicle.

Machine guns: Rifle-caliber small arms capable of automatic fire, used as primary or secondary armament of armored vehicles.

MBT: Main Battle Tank. MBTs are the primary tank type of modern armies, and combine characteristics of their medium and heavy tank ancestors.

MG: Machine Gun; also Maschinengewehr (German).

Muzzle brake: Device attached to the gun muzzle to reduce recoil force without seriously limiting muzzle velocity.

Muzzle velocity: Speed of projectile as it leaves the muzzle. Air friction means velocity drops rapidly once in flight.

Ordnance: Military equipment, specifically tube artillery.

Panzerkampfwagen: "Armored fighting vehicle" (German). Specifically tracked AFV or tank.

Panzerwagen: "Armored vehicle" (German).

Periscope: Optical device that enables viewer to see over obstacles. Enables tank crew to look out while remaining protected.

Rate of fire: Number of rounds that can be fired in a period of time, usually expressed in rounds per minute.

Reconnaissance vehicle: Mobile, lightly armored vehicle used for gathering battlefield intelligence.

RPG: Rocket Propelled Grenade Launcher. Soviet-made infantry antitank weapons.

Smoothbore: Cannon without rifling, designed to fire unrotated fin-stabilized projectiles.

Snorkel: Breather pipe delivering air to the engines of armored vehicles; allows vehicle to run submerged.

SPAAG: Self-Propelled Anti-Aircraft Gun system.

Spring: Part of suspension that absorbs vertical movement when on rough ground. It also enables the driven parts of the suspension to remain in contact with the ground.

Sturmpanzer: Assault armored vehicle (German). The name given to the first A7V tanks.

Tank destroyer: U.S. Army World War II lightly armored tracked vehicle armed with a powerful gun. Designed to ambush enemy armor.

Thermal imaging: Sensor system that detects heat generated by targets and projects it as a TV-style image onto a display screen.

Track: Endless belt circling the sprocket, idler, roadwheels and return rollers of a tracked suspension and providing the surface for the wheels to run on.

Transmission: Means by which the power of the engine is converted to rotary movement of wheels or tracks. Transmission can be hydraulic, mechanical, or electrical.

Traverse: The ability of a gun or turret to swing away from the centerline of a vehicle. A fully rotating turret has a traverse of 360 degrees.

Trench: Field fortification that the tank was developed to deal with. Expressed as a distance in feet or meters in a tank's specification, trench indicates the largest gap a tank can cross without being ditched.

Turret: Revolving armored box mounting a gun. Usually accommodates commander and other crew.

Velocity: The speed of a projectile at any point along its trajectory, usually measured in feet per second or meters per second.

Whippet: World War I term originally describing the first medium tanks, later to describe any light tank.

For More Information

American Armored Foundation, Inc.
Tank & Ordnance Museum
3401 U.S. highway 29B
Danville, VA 24540
(434) 836-5323
Web site: http://www.aaftankmuseum.com
This nonprofit organization collects, restores, preserves, and exhibits military tank artifacts from various nations and time periods.

American Military Museum
The Whittier Narrows Recreation Area
1918 Rosemead Boulevard
South El Monte, CA 91733
(626) 442-1776

Web site: http://www.tankland.com
This museum collects, preserves, restores, and exhibits military equipment.

The California State Military Museum
California State Military Department
1119 Second Street
Sacramento, CA 95814
(916) 856-1900
Web site: http://www.militarymuseum.org
This state museum houses more than 30,000 military artifacts.

Canadian War Museum
1 Vimy Place

Ottawa, ON K1A 0M8
Canada
(800) 555-5621
Web site: http://www.civilization.ca
This museum houses Canada's military artifacts, nearly 13,000 pieces, including a restored World War II Panther tank.

General George Patton Museum
4554 Fayette Avenue
Fort Knox, KY 40121-0208
(502) 624-3812
Web site: http://www.generalpatton.org
This museum and gallery offers exhibits on the legacy of General George Patton. There is also an online gallery that includes information about World War II and D-Day.

Military Museum of Southern New England
125 Park Avenue
Danbury, CT 06810
(203) 790-9277
Web site: http://www.usmilitarymuseum.org
This organization preserves U.S. military history, especially the American tank destroyer units of World War II.

Tank Museum
Bovington
Dorset, England BH20 6JG
United Kingdom
(+44) (0) 1929 405096

Web site: http://www.tankmuseum.org
The Tank Museum exhibits nearly 200 armored vehicles that have seen action in all major wars of the twentieth century.

U.S. Army Quartermaster Museum
1201 Twenty-second Street
Fort Lee, VA 23801
(804) 734-4203
Web site: http://www.qmmuseum.lee.army.mil/
This U.S. Army museum exhibits weaponry and historic artifacts at Fort Lee.

World Tank Museum
2625 Alcatraz Avenue #237
Berkeley, CA 94705
(510) 869-9941
Web site: http://www.world-tank-museum.com
This Web site offers detailed model replicas of historical tanks and armored fighting vehicles.

Web Sites

Due to the changing nature of Internet links, Rosen Publishing has developed an online list of Web sites related to the subject of this book. This site is updated regularly. Please use this link to access the list:

http://www.rosenlinks.com/wow/tanks

For Further Reading

Anderson, Christopher J. *Hell on Wheels: The Men of the U.S. Armed Forces, 1918 to the Present* (The G.I. Series). New York, NY: Chelsea House Publishers, 2001.

Bishop, Chris. *The Encyclopedia of Tanks and Armored Fighting Vehicles: From World War I to the Present Day.* San Diego, CA: Thunder Bay Press, 2006.

Browning, Peter. *The Changing Nature of Warfare: 1792–1945* (Cambridge Perspectives in History). Cambridge, UK: Cambridge University Press, 2002.

Chant, Christopher. *An Illustrated Data Guide to Battle Tanks of World War II* (Illustrated Data Guides). New York, NY: Chelsea House Publishers, 1997.

Edwards, John. *The Geeks of War: The Secretive Labs and Brilliant Minds Behind Tomorrow's Warfare Technologies.* New York, NY: AMACOM, 2005.

Gitlin, Martin. *George S. Patton: World War II General & Military Innovator.* Edina, MN: ABDO Publishing Company, 2010.

Green, Michael. *German Tanks of World War II.* Osceola, WI: MBI Publishing Company, 2000.

Green, Michael, and Greg Stewart. *Modern U.S. Tanks and AFVs.* St. Paul, MN: MBI Publishing Company, 2003.

Haskew, Michael E. *Postwar Armored Fighting Vehicles: 1945–Present* (Essential Vehicle Identification). London, UK: Amber Books, 2010.

Hatch, Alden. *General George Patton: Old Blood & Guts*. New York, NY: Sterling, 2006.

Jackson, Robert. *101 Great Tanks* (101 Greatest Weapons of All Times). New York, NY: Rosen Publishing Group, Inc., 2010.

Livesey, Jack. *Modern Armored Fighting Vehicles: From 1946 to the Present*. Leicester, UK: Anness, 2008.

Salecker, Gene Eric. *Rolling Thunder Against the Rising Sun: The Combat History of U.S. Army Tank Battalions in the Pacific in World War II*. Mechanicsburg, PA: Stackpole Books, 2008.

Watkins, Christine, ed. *Biological Warfare* (Opposing Viewpoints). Farmington Hills, MI: Greenhaven Press, 2010.

Yeide, Harry. *The Infantry's Armor: The U.S. Army's Separate Tank Battalions in World War II*. Mechanicsburg, PA: Stackpole Books, 2010.

Index

A

AAV7, 120–125
Afghanistan, 95, 101, 137
Afrika Korps, 6
AMX-13, 7, 80–85, 92
    DCA Anti-Aircraft, 83
AMX-30, 93
Starstreak, 153
Australia, 19, 61, 143

B

Barkmann, Ernst, 42–43
Blitzkrieg, 24
Britain, 5, 7, 12, 14, 16, 18, 33, 36, 48, 49, 56, 58, 60, 61, 87, 91, 92, 93, 108, 110, 112, 113, 114, 118, 130, 152, 153, 154, 155
Bulge, Battle of the, 25

C

Canada, 16, 137, 154
Centurion A41, 7, 56–60, 91, 100, 108, 112, 118
Challenger 2, 92, 93, 150–155
Char D'Assault St. Chamond, 11
Chieftain AVRE, 93, 111
Chieftain Mark 5, 93, 109–113
Chieftain 900, 93, 111
China, 63, 99, 122
Christie, Walter, 29
Cold War, 6, 50, 51, 54, 61, 66, 68, 72, 84, 86, 90, 93, 100, 112, 113
Czechoslovakia, 63, 97, 127, 131

D

D-Day, 37
Desert Rats, 6

E

El Alamein, Battle of, 36
Estienne, Jean-Baptiste Eugene, 11

F

Falklands War, 125
Forward Looking Infrared sighting, 143
France, 6, 7, 11, 12, 16, 80, 82, 84, 92, 93, 114, 144, 146, 148, 149
Fuller, J.F.C., 5, 19

G

Germany, 5, 6, 8–13, 19, 20, 22, 24, 25, 29, 30, 31, 32, 36, 37, 40, 42–43, 44, 46, 48, 51, 60, 81, 85, 93, 112, 114, 115, 116, 118, 119, 132, 133, 136, 137, 138, 144, 148, 154, 155
Greece, 115, 122
Guderian, Heinz, 6, 24, 30, 43
Gulf War, 94, 101, 125, 131, 143

H

Hitler, Adolf, 6, 7, 45
hoplites, 4

I

Indo-Pakistani War, 73, 94
Iran, 101, 109, 113
Iran-Iraq War, 91, 101
Iraq, 92, 95, 101, 125, 131, 143, 155
IS-3 Josef Stalin, 50–55
Israel, 59, 61, 73, 84, 91, 93, 94, 95, 131, 148
Italy, 115, 116, 118, 122

J

Japan, 54

K

Korean War, 61, 75, 78, 79
Kursk, Battle of, 39, 40, 43, 52

L

Leclerc, 144–149
Lend Lease, 36
Leonardo da Vinci, 4
Leopard 1, 91, 93, 112, 114–119, 132, 134
Leopard 2, 112, 119, 132–137, 138, 144, 154

M

M1A1 Abrams, 90, 92, 93, 95, 118, 136, 141, 142, 143, 144
M1A2 Abrams, 90, 93, 95, 138–143, 144
M4A4 Sherman, 32–37, 42, 49
M41 Walker Bulldog, 74–79
M48 Patton, 68–73, 86, 90, 93, 100, 118
M60, 86–91
M113, 102–107
    Dozer, 105
    Fitter, 105
M728 CEV, 89
Mark IV, 12, 19
Mark V
    Female, 19
    Male, 5, 14–19
Matilda, 110
Merkava, 93, 95
Montgomery, Bernard, 6

N

North Korea, 7, 97

O

Operation Desert Storm, 87, 91, 92
Operation Michael, 14

P

Panhard EBR armored car, 83
Panhard VBL scout car, 147
Panzerkampfwagen III, 22, 49
Panzerkampfwagen IV, 20–25, 30, 45
Panzerkampfwagen V Panther, 36, 38–43, 51, 81, 85
Panzerkampfwagen VI Tiger, 36, 44–50, 51
Patton, 7, 93
Patton, George S., 6, 72
Poland, 63, 127, 128, 131, 154

R

Reliability Improvements for Selected Equipment (RISE), 107
Renault VAB, 147
Ricardo, Harry, 19
Rommel, Erwin, 6
Russia, 6, 19, 26, 28, 30–31, 36, 38, 49, 50, 51, 52, 53, 54, 55, 62, 63, 64, 66, 68, 79, 86, 90, 91, 92, 93, 94, 96, 97, 98, 99, 100, 101, 108, 112, 126, 128, 130, 131

S

Schneider Char D'Assault, 11
Six-Day War, 61, 73, 94
Stalin, Josef, 6, 54
Sturmpanzerwagen A7V, 8–13

Sultan armored command
    vehicle, 153
Syria, 59, 101

T

T-34/85, 6, 26–31, 36, 49, 62,
    65, 130
T-54/55, 7, 59, 62–68, 79, 90,
    92, 96, 98, 99, 100, 112,
    129, 130
T-62, 59, 92, 96–101
T-64, 93, 98, 99, 100, 126, 127,
    128, 130
T-72, 92, 100, 126–131

Tank Urban Survival Kit
    (TUSK), 95, 143
Type 69, 99
Type 85/90, 141
Type 90, 141

U

United States, 7, 16, 19, 34, 36,
    42–43, 49, 61, 64, 70, 71,
    72, 73, 74, 75, 76, 78, 79,
    86, 89, 90, 92, 93, 94, 104,
    106, 118, 120, 122, 123,
    125, 132, 133, 136, 137,
    140, 143, 144, 148, 155

V

Versailles, Treaty of, 13
Vietnam War, 61, 69, 71, 73, 79,
    91, 103, 104, 105, 106, 107,
    123
Vollmer, Joseph, 11

W

Walker, Walton H., 75, 78
Wittmann, Michael, 48, 49
World War I, 5, 7, 12, 13, 14,
    16, 18
World War II, 5, 6, 20, 24, 25, 26,
    30–31, 32, 34, 35, 36, 37,

38, 39, 40, 41, 42–43, 44,
48, 49, 50, 51, 52, 53, 54,
55, 56, 57, 60–61, 62, 72,
74, 77, 78, 80, 81, 84, 85,
112, 118, 123, 130, 148, 152

X

XM-1 Abrams, 136, 137

Y

Yom Kippur War, 59, 61, 91, 94

Z

Zhukov, Georgi, 6

About the Author

Michael E. Haskew has been writing and researching military history subjects for more than twenty-five years. He is the editor of *WW II History Magazine* and the author of *The Sniper at War, Order of Battle: Western Allied Armies*, and *The Encyclopedia of Elite Forces in World War II*, and has contributed to numerous other books and periodicals. Haskew also served as editor of *The World War II Desk Reference* with the Eisenhower Center for American Studies. He lives in Chattanooga, Tennessee.